2013
The FBI Story

Hostage Rescue Team members debrief after a training exercise at their facility in Quantico, Virginia.

D1737691

JUN 1 2 2014
FEDERAL DEPOSITORY

A Message from FBI Director James B. Comey

This past year, the FBI and its partners again addressed a wide range of national security and criminal threats.

Together, we responded to numerous crisis incidents, such as the terrorist bombings of the Boston Marathon and the shootings at the Navy Yard in Washington, D.C. We confronted a continued surge of cyber attacks against targets ranging from everyday citizens to our largest and most successful businesses. And we stopped those who would strike at the heart of our communities—from violent gangs and white-collar criminals to child predators and corrupt public officials.

A glimpse of the challenges we faced—and what we achieved together—can be found in this latest edition of *The FBI Story*, our annual collection of news and feature articles from the Bureau's public website. Here you can read about some of our most successful recent major investigations and operations. These include a three-day nationwide sweep targeting child prostitution in which we identified and rescued more than 100 young victims and arrested more than 150 pimps; the rescue of a 5-year-old boy held captive in a heavily armed bunker in Alabama; and the uncovering of the largest domestic bribery and bid-rigging scheme in the history of federal contracting cases—one that siphoned more than $30 million dollars of taxpayer money.

Director James Comey delivers remarks at the White House following his nomination to lead the FBI on June 21, 2013. Director Comey was sworn in on September 4. (White House Photo)

This edition of *The FBI Story* also highlights some of the Bureau's remarkable capabilities. You will find a multi-part series on our elite Hostage Rescue Team—which marked its 30th anniversary this past year—and a feature on the Terrorist Explosive Device Analytical Center (TEDAC)—an FBI-established, multi-agency operation that celebrated its 10th anniversary in 2013.

For the FBI, 2013 was a year of transition, as my predecessor, Robert S. Mueller, III, completed his extraordinary 12-year tenure at the helm of the Bureau. Director Mueller guided the FBI in the aftermath of the September 11th attacks and spearheaded the Bureau's transformation into an intelligence-driven, threat-focused agency capable of confronting today's global security threats.

Following Bob Mueller is both a great challenge and a tremendous privilege. In my first months as Director, I have been meeting with our partners in the law enforcement and intelligence communities both in the United States and abroad. I want to ensure that we maintain open lines of communication about the work we are doing in our respective communities so that we can continue to build strong relationships to carry us into the future. Those same open and honest lines of communication are equally crucial for our private sector partners and the citizens we serve. I look forward to working with all of you in the months and years to come.

Thank you for your continued trust and support of the FBI, which we need to keep our country safe from harm.

James B Comey

Stopping a Suicide Bomber

Jihadist Planned Attack on U.S. Capitol

After months of consideration, a target was picked and a date was set: On February 17, 2012, Amine Mohamed El-Khalifi would strap on a bomb-laden vest and—in the name of jihad—blow himself up at an entrance to the U.S. Capitol. If anyone tried to stop him, he would shoot them with a MAC-10 assault weapon.

That's how the 29-year-old Northern Virginia resident believed events would unfold that Friday morning when he emerged from his car—suicide vest on and weapon by his side—in a parking garage near the Capitol.

"He totally believed he was going to die in the attack, and he seemed very much at peace with it," said a special agent on our Joint Terrorism Task Force (JTTF) who investigated the case. "The day of the attack, he was happy."

What El-Khalifi didn't know was that "Yusuf," the supposed al Qaeda operative he was conspiring with, was actually an undercover FBI agent—and the would-be terrorist's every move was being monitored by members of our Washington Field Office JTTF. Although El-Khalifi believed he was going to kill many people that day in the name of jihad, the explosives in his vest and the assault weapon had been rendered inoperable by FBI technicians.

A Moroccan citizen who came to the U.S. more than a decade ago, El-Khalifi initially embraced Western culture. But in 2010 he began posting radical jihadist messages online and expressed an interest in joining the mujahedeen to fight in Afghanistan. "As far as we know," said the special agent who investigated El-Khalifi, "he became radicalized online."

In January 2011, El-Khalifi met with individuals in a Washington suburb where jihad was endorsed and weapons were displayed. By the end of 2011—after he had been introduced to our undercover agent—El-Khalifi was actively seeking to join an armed extremist group, and he suggested bombing attacks on targets ranging from a local synagogue to a restaurant frequented by U.S. military officials.

During meetings with our undercover agent, El-Khalifi handled weapons and explosives and said he would use a gun to kill people face-to-face. Finally, in January 2012, after a test explosion in a West Virginia quarry (carefully monitored by the JTTF), El-Khalifi decided to attack the Capitol building. It would be a suicide mission.

Over the next month, the would-be bomber visited the Capitol building several times to conduct surveillance. On the morning of February 17, El-Khalifi drove to the parking garage and put on the suicide vest. As he walked toward the Capitol, he was quickly arrested.

Four months later, El-Khalifi pled guilty to attempted use of a weapon of mass destruction. In September, he was sentenced to 30 years in prison.

"This case ended well, thanks to the work of the JTTF," our agent said. "All our JTTF partners, including state and local law enforcement, played a key role. It's scary to consider this guy's intentions," the agent added. "He was totally rational. There was no disconnect from reality—he was going to kill people and he felt that was the right way to express his religious beliefs."

The agent noted that one of El-Khalifi's original plans was to take an automatic weapon to a shopping mall and shoot as many people as possible. "It's frightening to think what might have happened if he had not shown up on the FBI's radar."

Left: One of six CART mobile labs with state-of-the-art capabilities for acquiring, processing, and analyzing digital evidence…even while the vehicle is in motion.

Piecing Together Digital Evidence
The Computer Analysis Response Team

In a case involving the round-up of dozens of suspects indicted on public corruption and other charges, investigators were faced with processing large numbers of seized cell phones, desktop computers, and laptops belonging to the suspects. In another case, key evidence against a terror suspect arrested for attempted use of a weapon of mass destruction included data found on his computer. And after a U.S. congresswoman was wounded and six people killed in Arizona, vital evidence was found on security camera footage, computers, and cell phones.

Reflecting a trend that has become increasingly commonplace for law enforcement, all three of these cases involved the need to recover digital evidence. And our Computer Analysis Response Team, or CART, is the FBI's go-to force for providing digital forensic services not only to our own investigators but also in some instances to our local, state, and federal partners.

CART consists of nearly 500 highly trained and certified special agents and other professional personnel working at FBI Headquarters, throughout our 56 field offices, and within the network of Regional Computer Forensics Laboratories across the nation. They analyze a variety of digital media—including desktop and laptop computers, CDs/DVDs, cell phones, digital cameras, digital media players, flash media, etc.—lawfully seized as part of our investigations.

During fiscal year 2012, CART—while supporting nearly 10,400 investigations—conducted more than 13,300 digital forensic examinations involving more than 10,500 terabytes of data. To put that last figure into perspective, it's widely believed that the total printed content in the Library of Congress is equal to about 10 terabytes of data.

CART examiners are experts at extracting data from digital media…even when the media is damaged by the forces of nature or by defendants attempting to prevent data from being recovered.

The cases that CART examiners work span the gamut of FBI program areas: from cyber crimes and computer intrusions to violent crimes, financial crimes, organized crime, and national security matters. And once they have finished their forensic work, CART examiners are also available to testify in court as expert witnesses on their findings.

Because we come across computers and other digital media so often in the course of our investigative work, our CART examiners can't possibly handle every piece of media. That's why CART created a basic digital evidence training course and developed easy-to-use examination tools for field investigators—to give them the technical and legal knowledge they need to process simpler and more basic digital evidence from their cases without altering or damaging the data—which allow CART examiners to focus on more technically complex cases.

CART on the go. While much of CART's work is done in stationary facilities in the field or back at our national Headquarters, we also have six mobile CART laboratories around the country. These mobile labs are especially valuable when time is of the essence, enabling digital evidence to be examined on the spot.

CART…an evidence response team for today's high-tech environment.

Human Trafficking Awareness
Targeting Traffickers, Helping Victims

Last month, a Kentucky cardiologist and his ex-wife pled guilty to recruiting a Bolivian woman to work as their domestic servant and holding her unlawfully for nearly 15 years. The couple took her passport, threatened her with deportation, and falsely promised that her wages were being put in a bank account.

Trafficking in persons is a widespread form of modern-day slavery, and as we observe National Slavery and Human Trafficking Prevention Month, we'd like to update you on what the FBI—with its partners—is doing to go after the traffickers and help the victims.

Human trafficking is a top investigative priority of the Bureau's civil rights program. During fiscal year 2012, we opened 306 human trafficking investigations around the nation involving forced labor or forced household service as well as sex trafficking of international victims (young and old) and adult U.S. citizen victims.

Along the same lines, the sex trafficking of U.S. children is also a priority within our Violent Crimes Against Children program. During fiscal year 2012, we opened 363 investigations into the commercial sexploitation of domestic minors. Fortunately, we were also able to locate more than 500 young victims of sex traffickers.

We participate in 88 human trafficking task forces and working groups around the country. Our efforts include not only investigating cases where we find them but also proactively using intelligence to drive and support these cases, looking at known areas of human trafficking activities, and developing liaison relationships within communities to promote awareness of these crimes.

Help for victims. The Bureau also has a robust assistance program in place for victims of human trafficking and other federal crimes investigated by the FBI. Our Office for Victim Assistance (OVA) oversees the work of victim specialists located throughout our 56 field offices.

These specialists—experienced in crisis intervention, social services, and victim assistance—work closely with agents to ensure that potential victims of trafficking are rescued, transferred to safe locations, and provided with referrals for medical, mental health, housing, legal, and other necessary services. And this past year,

representatives from OVA and our civil rights program developed a protocol for human trafficking investigations that was implemented in all FBI field offices. The protocol highlights a victim-centered approach and the need for collaboration between the investigating agent, the local victim specialist, non-governmental agencies, and other law enforcement partners.

OVA oversees our child/adolescent forensic interviewers who work with Violent Crimes Against Children task forces and provide training for agents and task force officers working human trafficking cases. These interviewers also collaborated with partner agencies to develop an interview protocol for minor victims of sexploitation for use by professionals working against human trafficking.

Our training and awareness efforts were significant. During fiscal year 2012, we conducted training around the country focused on defining, detecting, and investigating human trafficking cases. The audiences included law enforcement (both U.S. and international) along with government employees, religious and civic organizations, ethnic advocacy groups, schools, social service agencies, medical personnel, legal aid agencies, domestic violence services, etc.—in short, anyone in a position to make a difference in the life of a trafficking victim.

Multi-agency investigations, intelligence, victim assistance, training—we're putting our tools and capabilities to work to help combat the scourge of human trafficking.

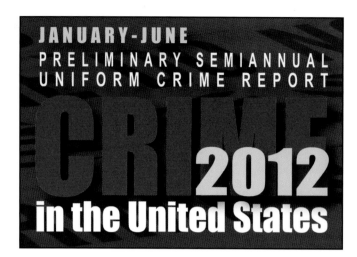

Early 2012 Crime Stats
Slight Uptick in Crime

According to statistics from our *Preliminary Semiannual Uniform Crime Report, January-June 2012*, the number of violent crimes reported by law enforcement for the first six months of 2012 increased 1.9 percent over figures from the same period in 2011. Property crimes also rose 1.5 percent overall.

Violent Crime. Two of the four offenses in the violent crime category actually showed overall decreases when compared with data from the first six months of 2011—murders dropped 1.7 percent and forcible rapes fell 1.4 percent. But the number of robberies increased 2.0 percent and aggravated assaults 2.3 percent.

At a regional level, the West saw the largest overall jump in violent crime—up 3.1 percent—followed by a rise of 2.5 percent in the Midwest and 1.1 percent each in the South and the Northeast. Despite these increases, the number of murders fell 4.8 percent in the South and 2.4 percent in the Northeast.

The only violent crime offense category that showed increases in all four regions of the country was aggravated assault, which was up 4.4 percent in the Midwest, 2.4 percent in the West, 1.7 percent in the South, and 0.8 percent in the Northeast.

Property crime. On the property crime front, all three offense categories showed overall increases—1.9 percent for larceny-theft, 1.7 percent for motor vehicle theft, and 0.1 percent for burglary.

Regionally, the West saw the largest rise in property crime—up 4.7 percent, followed closely by the Northeast at 4.0 percent. The Midwest was up 1.3 percent, but the South actually showed a decrease of 1.4 percent.

For individual property crime offense categories, statistics indicate that the West had the largest increase in the number of burglaries (up 6.7 percent) and motor vehicle thefts (up 8.1 percent). And the Northeast had the largest rise in the number of larceny-thefts, which were up 4.5 percent.

The statistics for arson, collected separately from other property crimes because of varying degrees of reporting among law enforcement agencies, showed an overall jump of 3.2 percent during the first six months of 2012. Three of the four regions of the country reported increases—up 11.0 percent in the Midwest, 6.4 percent in the West, and 5.7 percent in the Northeast. The South saw a 5.6 decrease in arson offenses.

New offense categories. On the heels of National Slavery and Human Trafficking Awareness Month this January, our Uniform Crime Reporting (UCR) Program will begin collecting human trafficking data this year in two categories—commercial sex acts and involuntary servitude. The William Wilberforce Trafficking Victims Protection Reauthorization Act of 2008 requires the data collection, and with input from our law enforcement partners, the UCR Program began developing specific definitions and data collection guidelines for these offenses. Stay tuned for more details on implementation.

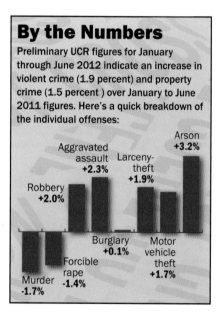

Preliminary crime stats for the full year—contained in UCR's *Preliminary Annual Uniform Crime Report, January-December 2012*—should be available in six months, and final figures are scheduled to be released by the end of the year.

Murder-for-Hire
Web Hits of a Deadly Kind

Marissa Mark wanted someone dead—her ex-boyfriend's new girlfriend, to be precise. And she found a way to have it done…from her computer.

In September 2006, the Pennsylvania resident and recent college graduate logged on to HitmanForHire.net, a site often misinterpreted as a joke. But it was no laughing matter for Mark, who spelled it out very clearly: "I…want her done by [a] shot to the head."

And the "hitman for hire" on the other end? Las Vegas poker dealer Essam Ahmed Eid, an Egyptian national who was apparently looking for a little something to do on the side. After demanding a $37,000 fee from Mark—who came up with a "down payment" by stealing credit card information she had access to at the collections agency where she worked—Eid drove to the Los Angeles area, where he showed up at the workplace of the 23-year-old intended victim.

Eid presented the young woman with a dossier of sorts—photos of her, e-mails concerning the plan—and then paused. "You remind me of my daughter," he said. He told the victim she could have three days to pay off the contract, and he would let her live. Panicked, she notified authorities.

The case went to Special Agent Ingerd Sotelo, from the FBI's Los Angeles Field Office. Sotelo discussed the particulars with the victim and had her make recorded phone calls pleading for more time to come up with the money…but Eid went radio silent.

Having identified Eid by this point and acting on a hunch that he had fled the country, Sotelo traced Eid to Ireland. She learned that he had recently been arrested for burglary and extortion, but thought there might be more to it than that—she was right. Eid had crossed the pond and committed those crimes because of another hit ordered through his website—and smuggled in homemade ricin in his contact lens case, to boot.

Murder-for-hire with an interstate nexus became a federal crime in 1958, but our involvement in these cases goes back at least to the 1930s and the days of the notorious Mafia hit squad Murder, Inc. And—according to Special Agent Janelle Miller, head of our Violent Crimes Unit—they're more common than you might think, "We do a lot of them," she said; 140 cases not tied to organized crime are currently pending, many

of which involve inmates. "The names change, the story doesn't," said Miller, "but there is a threshold. It can't just be, 'I'm going to kill my lawyer,' and that's it."

Sotelo agrees. "A lot of people might say they want someone dead," she explained, "but unless you do something to put it in action, you haven't committed a crime."

As for Eid…after serving a six-year prison term in Ireland, he was extradited to the U.S., where he pled guilty to extortion charges and was sentenced in 2011 to 33 months in prison. And Mark received six years for ordering the hit and using stolen credit cards.

But did Eid kill anyone? "I never could find that he actually did," said Sotelo, "but he had all the stuff he needed," including a pistol with a silencer, a castor bean plant, and a ricin recipe (he had also attempted to order cyanide). Thankfully, he never got to use it.

Left: One of the Detroit facilities used by Quality Recreation and Rehabilitation, Inc. (QRR), which became Procare after Medicare questioned QRR's submitted claims.

Abuse of Trust
Mentally Disabled Used to Scam Government

It's hard to believe…a longtime Detroit doctor taking advantage of severely mentally disabled adults to line his own pocket.

Earlier this month, Dr. Alphonso Berry and two criminal colleagues—a married couple named Marcus and Beth Jenkins—pled guilty to defrauding the government by submitting more than $13.2 million worth of phony claims to Medicare over a seven-year period for group and individual psychotherapy sessions that were never provided.

How the scam operated. In 2004, Marcus and Beth Jenkins incorporated Quality Recreation and Rehabilitation (QRR), an adult day care center that claimed to provide psychotherapy services. At the same time, they also operated adult foster care homes in the Detroit area that provided 24-hour personal care, protection, and supervision for individuals who were—for the most part—mentally or physically disabled. The couple obtained Medicare provider numbers for QRR and clinicians working on staff, including Dr. Alphonso Berry.

For four years, the Jenkinses transported Medicare beneficiaries residing at adult foster care homes (both theirs and others) to QRR, and, in concert with Dr. Berry—who often signed patient progress charts and progress notes for individual and group psychotherapy sessions—submitted claims to Medicare for psychotherapy services for these beneficiaries that were never provided. The funds received from Medicare—approximately $1.8 million—were diverted from QRR's bank accounts into the hands of the Jenkinses and Dr. Berry.

Then, around June 2008, QRR received notice from Medicare questioning its submitted claims and the legitimacy of its psychotherapy services. But rather than shut down their fraudulent scheme, Marcus and Beth Jenkins simply opened a new adult day care facility called Procare a few months later, which also supposedly offered psychotherapy services. Again, the Jenkinses would transport Medicare patients from adult foster care homes to Procare, and Dr. Berry would sign patient charts and notes. Over the next four years, approximately $6.5 million more in phony claims were submitted; Medicare ended up paying Procare approximately $2.5 million on those claims. And once again, the funds were diverted into the hands of the Jenkinses and Dr. Berry, who spent the money on lavish lifestyles.

The case began in October 2010, when the U.S. Department of Health and Human Services (HHS) received a referral based on an unusually high number of hours being billed per day by Dr. Berry (sometimes surpassing 24 hours in one day). HHS reached out to the FBI, and we soon began investigating with our partners from HHS' Office of Inspector General. We examined financial records. We interviewed QRR and Procare office staff, the Medicare beneficiaries, and social workers. And we conducted surveillance of the suspects.

In October 2011, our evidence led to indictments against Dr. Berry and Marcus and Beth Jenkins. The case was brought as part of the Medicare Fraud Strike Force, operating in nine cities across the country and composed of interagency teams of analysts, investigators, and prosecutors who target fraud.

And what of the Medicare beneficiaries living in the Jenkinses' adult foster care homes? They are being moved to other facilities, where they will get the care and medical treatment they are entitled to.

A Byte Out of History
The Alger Hiss Story

The jury returned from its deliberations on January 21, 1950—63 years ago this month. The verdict? Guilty on two counts of perjury.

Alger Hiss, a well-educated and well-connected former government lawyer and State Department official who helped create the United Nations in the aftermath of World War II, was headed to prison in Atlanta for lying to a federal grand jury.

The central issue of the trial was espionage. In August 1948, Whittaker Chambers—a senior editor at *Time* magazine—was called by the House Committee on Un-American Activities to corroborate the testimony of Elizabeth Bentley, a Soviet spy who had defected in 1945 and accused dozens of members of the U.S. government of espionage. One official she named as possibly connected to the Soviets was Alger Hiss.

The FBI immediately began probing her claims to ensure those who were credibly named—including Hiss—did not continue to have access to government secrets or power. As the investigation into Bentley and related matters deepened in 1946 and 1947, Congress became aware of and concerned about the case. Details leaked to the press, and the investigation became national news and embroiled in partisan politics in the run up to the 1948 presidential election.

Chambers, who had renounced the Communist Party in the late 1930s, testified reluctantly that hot summer day. He ultimately acknowledged he was part of the communist underground in the 1930s and that Hiss and others had been members of the group.

In later testimony, Hiss vehemently denied the accusation. After all, Chambers had offered no proof that Hiss had committed espionage or been previously connected to Bentley or the communist group.

It could have ended there, but members of the committee—especially then-California Congressman Richard Nixon—prodded Chambers into disclosing information suggesting there was more to his story and his relationship with Hiss. In later testimony, Hiss admitted knowing Chambers in the 1930s, but he continued to deny any ties to communism and later filed a libel suit against his accuser.

Alger Hiss was convicted in January 1950.

The committee was torn. Who was telling the truth, Hiss or Chambers? And should either be charged with perjury?

A key turn of events came in November 1948, when Chambers produced documents showing both he and Hiss were committing espionage. Then, in early December, Chambers provided the committee with a package of microfilm and other information he had hidden inside a pumpkin on his Maryland farm. The two revelations, which became known as the "Pumpkin Papers," contained images of State Department materials—including notes in Hiss' own handwriting.

It was the smoking gun the Justice Department needed. Hiss was charged with perjury; he could not be indicted for espionage because the statute of limitations had run out. An extensive FBI investigation helped develop a great deal of evidence verifying Chambers' statements and revealing Hiss' cover-ups.

In 1949, the first trial resulted in a hung jury, but in 1950, Hiss was convicted. Sixty-three years ago today, he was sentenced to five years in prison, ending an important case that helped further confirm the increasing penetration of the U.S. government by the Soviets during the Cold War.

FBI en Español
Spanish Language Webpage Turns 2

Two years ago this month, we enhanced our outreach to the Hispanic community in the U.S.—and beyond—by launching a Spanish-language webpage on www.fbi.gov.

Our goal—to help educate members of the Hispanic community about the FBI's many roles and responsibilities in fighting crime…to enlist more support in locating fugitives and gathering tips on criminal activity…and to provide valuable information on how to keep from becoming a victim of fraud or other crimes.

So far, the site has been viewed more than 160,000 times. More importantly, by strategically syndicating content from the webpage to various online Spanish-language media outlets in the U.S., our regular stream of articles tailored to Hispanics reached a combined audience of more than 70 million people during 2012 alone.

Over the past two years, we have posted stories on a variety of topics of interest to the Hispanic community…as well as to the public at large. For example:

- In our latest article, we discussed human trafficking (January is National Slavery and Human Trafficking Prevention Month) with a focus on the assistance we offer to human trafficking victims.

- Last April, we warned about the increasing sophistication of the so-called "grandparent scam," in which criminals can—using the Internet and social media sites—uncover personal information about their targets, which makes the scam so much more believable.

- Last January, we warned people about new malware being delivered via e-mail that made it possible for criminals to steal money electronically from victims' bank accounts.

- And in March 2011, we provided details on a California con man who ran a Ponzi scheme and a distressed homeowners scam, both specifically targeting members of the Hispanic community in Los Angeles.

Over the past 24 months, we've also run articles covering topics such as gangs and gang violence, hate crimes, telemarketing fraud, mortgage and health care fraud, cyber crime, sextortion, child prostitution, ATM skimming, identity theft, and the FBI Child ID app.

Along with our Spanish-language webpage, FBI.gov provides some additional Spanish content as well, including a number of posters on our Most Wanted fugitives page, key forms, and a translation of the authorized language on the FBI's Anti-Piracy Warning Seal.

Our Spanish webpage is just one example of how we reach out to the Hispanic community. Our Community Relations Unit at FBI Headquarters—which directs the Bureau's overall outreach efforts—oversees the work of our community outreach specialists in FBI field offices across the country. Our specialists interact at the local level with leaders, groups, and others in the Hispanic community, sharing information and engaging in meaningful dialogue. They also facilitate the participation of Hispanics in our Citizens Academy and CREST programs as well as our Director's Community Leadership Awards.

"Our outreach efforts are all about connecting with communities to make sure they know who we are and how we can help," says Paul Geiger, chief of our Community Relations Unit. "We want to be better at our job and keep the public safer. The Spanish-language webpage certainly helps do that."

Stay tuned for more interesting and useful content on FBI en español during 2013.

The Hostage Rescue Team
Part 1: 30 Years of Service to the Nation

Last month marked the 30th anniversary of the FBI's Hostage Rescue Team (HRT)—federal law enforcement's only full-time counterterrorism unit—a highly trained group of special agents often called upon during the toughest times.

When needed, the team is prepared to deploy within four hours of notification to anywhere in the U.S. in response to terrorist incidents, hostage situations, and major criminal threats. Although the HRT has been tasked to fill a variety of roles throughout the years, its highest priority has always been to react to a major terrorist incident and to ensure the safe release of hostages.

"There is no greater mission we have than to save somebody's life," said Kevin Cornelius, a former HRT operator who now commands the team.

Although the HRT was originally conceived to provide a tactical response to terrorism, the team possesses capabilities that do not exist anywhere else in civilian law enforcement. Operators are able to fast-rope out of helicopters, parachute with full mission equipment, and conduct advanced SCUBA techniques. They are trained to be superior marksmen, proficient in a variety of breaching techniques—including explosives—and experts in close-quarter tactics. Each operator's skill and training ensures that the HRT can launch assaults with speed, precision, and, if necessary, deadly force.

U.S. law enforcement relies on a tiered response to critical incidents such as a terrorist attack or hostage situation. First responders usually come from the local and state level and might include SWAT teams and crisis negotiators. If a situation cannot be resolved at that level, federal assets such as the HRT may be called in.

HRT operators also provide technical and tactical assistance to FBI field offices, which often leads to the apprehension of violent offenders. Most of the HRT's operations in the U.S. occur as a result of detailed investigations conducted by special agents in the field.

Since the first generation of HRT operators were trained in 1983, team members have deployed domestically and around the globe nearly 800 times,

HRT members debrief after a training exercise at their facility in Quantico, Virginia.

putting themselves in harm's way to help safeguard the nation and to save lives.

"As an elite counterterrorism tactical team for law enforcement, the HRT is one of the best—if not the best—in the United States," said Sean Joyce, deputy director of the FBI and former HRT operator. "They are elite because of their training," he explained. "But they are FBI agents first and foremost, and they have the ability to perform special agent duties—whether it's obtaining evidence or interviewing an individual—anywhere in the world while being able to operate in all types of environments, no matter how inhospitable."

Not surprisingly, it takes a certain kind of special agent to become an HRT operator. In its 30-year existence, fewer than 300 individuals have been selected to join the team. Those who make it possess remarkable physical and mental toughness. They may be capable of extraordinary individual effort, but they understand the team always comes first—even before their own personal needs. Identifying candidates who possess not only the necessary physical and tactical abilities but also the right combination of personality traits is an integral part of the team's demanding selection process.

Part 2: Trying out for the team (page 12)

Scan this **QR code** with your smartphone to access related video and photos, or visit www.fbi.gov/hrtanniversary.

A Case of 'Sextortion'
Cons Like 'Bieber Ruse' Targeted Minor Girls

The basic framework of the extortionist's scheme was as cold as it was calculated: contact a young girl on a social networking site using a fake identity, gain her trust, extract some highly personal information, and then threaten to expose her intimate exchanges if she doesn't assent to escalating demands for sexually explicit pictures or videos.

The case of Christopher Patrick Gunn, 31, of Montgomery, Alabama, who was sentenced last month to 35 years in prison for producing child pornography through a massive online sextortion scheme, provides a glimpse of how modern-day confidence men are plying their trade against the most vulnerable and unsuspecting victims. By trolling social media networks and lurking in video chats, Gunn was able to reach out to hundreds of young girls and set his bait. In methodically scripted ruses, friendly conversations would turn personal, with Gunn asking girls about their bra sizes, their sexual histories, and other intimate details. If the girls sent pictures, Gunn demanded more revealing images. If they complied, he set the hook some more, threatening to destroy their reputations by publishing their compromising images, videos, and correspondence.

This is a common thread in sextortion schemes, say FBI special agents who investigate these cases.

"Once he started in, he got to know everything about the girls—their friends' names, their schools, their parents' names—it was like a script," said Erik Doell, a special agent in the FBI's Montgomery, Alabama office who investigated the Gunn case. "Once he got a picture, the girls would just go along with it. They would do whatever they could to keep their reputations intact."

In one wrenching case, revealed through transcripts read at Gunn's sentencing hearing in January, a 13-year-old victim pleaded that she did not want to take her shirt off in front of a webcam. She told Gunn she had "a life, please do not ruin it," before ultimately relenting to his demands.

To gain the girls' trust, Gunn primarily used two ruses:

- In the "**new kid ruse**," Gunn created a fake profile on Facebook and claimed in messages to minors that he was a new kid in town looking to make friends. Once he established a level of trust, he began making demands.

- In the "**Justin Bieber ruse**," Gunn pretended to be the teen pop star on several interactive video chat services. When Gunn convinced girls he was the singer, he offered them free concert tickets or backstage passes in exchange for topless photos or webcam videos.

Gunn employed these tactics for more than two years, victimizing girls in at least a half-dozen states and Ireland. The case came to light in April 2011, when junior high school students in a small town in Alabama complained to local police about requests for sexually explicit pictures they received on Facebook. Separate police investigations in Mississippi and Louisiana uncovered strikingly similar details. Drawing from the police investigations, the FBI searched Gunn's home, where a cellphone and laptop computer revealed the massive scope and novel ruses of Gunn's extortion scheme.

In Gunn's case, the scheme came to light only after kids and their parents reported his advances. Special Agent Doell said there may be more victims in the case who never came forward. And certainly there are more extortion artists like Gunn preying on kids' natural naiveté.

"Kids live in a wired world," Doell said. "They don't think twice about taking a picture and sending it to someone. A Polaroid could only go so far. But on the Internet, it's out there for the world."

Amish Beard-Cutting Case
Ohio Residents Sentenced for Hate Crimes

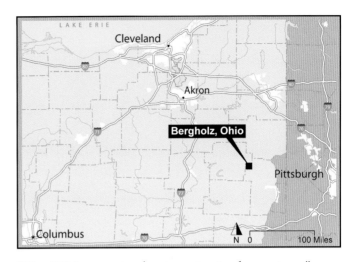

Sixteen individuals were sentenced today for hate crimes involving attacks against Amish residents in Ohio—some carried out by the victims' children—and the group's leader received a 15-year prison term.

In response to a religious dispute among members of the Amish community, Samuel Mullet, Sr.—the 66-year-old bishop of the Amish congregation in Bergholz, Ohio—directed his followers to forcibly cut the hair and beards of other members of the Amish faith.

Male and female victims, some elderly, were held against their will in their homes while scissors and horse shears were used to cut their hair and beards. Head and facial hair is religiously symbolic to the Amish—some of the male victims had been growing their beards for decades.

"These crimes were definitely religiously motivated," said Michael Sirohman, the special agent in our Cleveland Field Office who investigated the case. Mullet and his Bergholz followers practiced a different kind of religion than other Amish communities, and Mullet believed those other communities were against him and were interfering with his authority. That was the underlying reason for the attacks, Sirohman said.

"Sam Mullet didn't like to be crossed," he explained, "and he was very good at manipulating his followers." Mullet convinced the individuals who carried out the attacks that they were religiously permitted to do so, Sirohman added. "In some perverted way, they thought they were helping the victims by bringing them closer to God."

Mullet organized five attacks between September and November 2011. Local authorities filed state charges against him and others after the initial incidents, but the assaults continued. The FBI and the U.S. Attorney's Office were called in, Sirohman said, because the attacks were escalating and because "everyone realized there were bigger issues involved."

Hate crimes are investigated under the FBI's civil rights program, and the passage of the Matthew Shepard and James Byrd, Jr., Hate Crimes Prevention Act in 2009 gave the Bureau further authority to investigate such offenses.

"The FBI is committed to investigating hate crimes," said Stephen Anthony, special agent in charge of our Cleveland Field Office, "including those motivated by religious bias—as in this case—or other areas protected by our civil rights statutes."

Although the Amish attacks were brazen, victims were initially reluctant to come forward, in part because the Amish community is insulated from mainstream society. Ultimately, Sirohman said, the victims cooperated "because they didn't want this to happen to other people."

The FBI received "outstanding" assistance from local sheriff's departments and the U.S. Attorney's Office for the Northern District of Ohio, Sirohman said, and in November 2011, Mullet, members of his family, and other followers were arrested. Last September, they were convicted of hate crimes and other charges.

Sirohman had special praise for the victims in the case. "They were very brave," he said. "In many cases they had to testify against their own children." He was also gratified that the victims, who do not easily associate with those outside of their faith, recognized the help that the FBI and federal prosecutors were offering.

"They trusted us to do what was right," Sirohman added, "and we weren't going to let them down."

The Hostage Rescue Team
Part 2: The Crucible of Selection

FBI agents hoping to earn a spot on the Hostage Rescue Team—federal law enforcement's lead counterterrorism tactical team—relinquish their names when they report for the grueling selection process held at Quantico, Virginia each year.

During two exhausting weeks of tests and drills that purposely induce physical and mental stress, candidates are known to their evaluators only as "selectees," and the only thing that distinguishes them from one another is an identifying color and number worn on their clothes. It is all part of the process that helps evaluators choose the very best individuals for one of the most demanding—and rewarding—jobs in the FBI.

"The process is designed to identify individuals who will perform the best in a crisis situation," said FBI Deputy Director Sean Joyce, a former HRT operator. "The point is to break you down to see how you perform under stress. When you don't get a lot of sleep—sometimes going on one or two hours a day—over a period of time, it's going to break you down pretty quickly."

On the first day, candidates are roused well before dawn for physical fitness tests that include running, swimming, and stair-climbing with a 55-pound vest and 35-pound battering ram—all with little rest between activities. "The first day is the easy day," said Special Agent John Piser, a former HRT operator who runs the selection process.

Punishing runs while carrying heavy gear, along with drills carried out in high places, cramped quarters, and other unforgiving circumstances are the norm during

Left: HRT "selectees" are distinguishable during selection only by number and the color of their clothes.

selection. Being in peak physical condition is critical, but candidates must also perform well on firearms tests and during complex arrest scenarios. Equally important is showing good judgment, thinking on your feet, and being a team player—despite being sleep-deprived and physically drained.

"You can be the fastest person in the world, the strongest person in the world, or the smartest person in the world," Joyce explained, "but if you're not willing to be a part of the team, you don't belong on HRT."

In addition to being able to work with others, evaluators are looking for other core personality characteristics such as loyalty, leadership, and discipline. And during the two-week trial, selectees have no idea how they are doing.

"They get zero feedback," Piser said. "No negative or positive. We give them a task, and it's on them to perform. We tell them that all events are evaluated and to give it 100 percent." That can be tough on certain personalities, he added. "They want that feedback, and we give them nothing." It's another way to test mental toughness.

Typically, about half of every class drops out for various reasons during the selection process. Even if a person is still standing at the end of two weeks, Piser said, that is no guarantee he will make the team. "Just surviving is not enough."

Part 3: The real training begins (page 14)

Crooked CEO Gets 50 Years
Stole $215 Million from Investors

He was a successful CEO of his own futures brokerage firm and a respected member of his community, creating jobs and supporting local charities.

Or so it seemed. For years, Russell Wasendorf, Sr.—as Acting U.S. Attorney Sean R. Berry of the Northern District of Iowa recently put it—was really a "con man who built a business on smoke and mirrors."

It all fell apart in July 2012, when Wasendorf—after an unsuccessful suicide attempt—admitted stealing millions from more than 13,000 investors who had entrusted their hard-earned money to him and his company, the now-bankrupt Peregrine Financial Group (PFG), based in Cedar Falls, Iowa. Last month, Wasendorf was sentenced by a federal judge to 50 years in prison—the maximum term allowed by law—and ordered to pay restitution to his victims.

How it started. In the early 1990s, Wasendorf's Peregrine partner pulled his money out of the operation, and Wasendorf didn't have the funds to keep the company going. So he helped himself to at least $250,000 of Peregrine's customer funds in accounts at an outside bank. To conceal the theft, he used a copy machine to fabricate a phony bank statement.

For the next 20 or so years, Wasendorf continued to steal from customer funds while his company incurred tens of millions of dollars in losses. He carried out this scheme through a series of complex actions designed to conceal his activities and the deteriorating state of the company. For instance:

- He maintained exclusive control of monthly bank statements by instructing PFG personnel to make sure they were delivered to him unopened. He then used a copy machine—and later, computer software—to create phony monthly statements in place of the real statements.

- He sent the phony statements to PFG's accounting department, knowing they'd be used in various reports required by oversight bodies—the Commodity Futures Trading Commission (CFTC) and the National Futures Association (NFA).

The $20 million headquarters of the now-bankrupt Peregrine Financial Group in Cedar Falls, Iowa.

- He intercepted account verification forms from NFA and CFTC auditors mailed to the bank used by PFG. Wasendorf changed the address of the bank to a post office box that only he had access to; once the forms came into that post office box, he would mail back to the auditors a forged form—supposedly from the bank—that contained an inflated dollar amount of what was in the corresponding bank account.

What did Wasendorf do with the misappropriated funds? He created the appearance that PFG was legitimate and successful in order to ward off the suspicions of regulators and auditors. He also funded his own outside business interests—for example, he opened two restaurants in Cedar Falls. And finally, he lived quite luxuriously—he owned a private jet and a huge estate that included a million-dollar indoor swimming pool and a 1,000-bottle wine cellar.

The case began when the Blackhawk County Sheriff's Office, first on the scene of Wasendorf's attempted suicide, contacted the FBI after discovering notes left by the executive admitting his illegal deeds. The ensuing federal investigation—which involved multiple searches, reviews of thousands of electronic and paper documents, and numerous interviews—culminated in September 2012 with Wasendorf's guilty plea.

Special thanks as well to our partners at the U.S. Postal Inspection Service and the U.S. Attorney's Office for the Northern District of Iowa for their assistance in this case.

The Hostage Rescue Team
Part 3: Training for Every Contingency

The handful of special agents who make it through the Hostage Rescue Team's selection process have only just begun their journey to become HRT operators. Each new generation of recruits must undergo eight months of intensive training before joining the team and deploying on missions.

"As an HRT operator, you are going to be on the cutting edge of what the Bureau does tactically, both in the United States and overseas," said Special Agent John Piser, a former operator who now runs the team's selection and training programs. "That requires a substantial commitment—and a significant amount of training."

Recruits relocate to be near the HRT's headquarters in Quantico, Virginia. There, they begin New Operator Training School—a full-time job and a total immersion into the world of tactics, firearms, and teamwork.

Over the course of 32 weeks, new operators learn specialized skills—fast-roping out of helicopters and SCUBA diving, for example—and few are more critical than close-quarter battle (CQB). "How quickly we can secure a house with a credible threat inside might mean the difference between a hostage living or dying," Piser said.

As new operators advance in tactical expertise, training drills become more complex. Live-fire CQB exercises in the HRT's "shooting house" mimic real-world missions. The shooting house is a large, maze-like series of rubber-coated walls—the rubber absorbs bullets and prevents ricocheting—that can be arranged into different room configurations so a variety of scenarios can be played out. As operators work together to effect a successful resolution, instructors view their movements from catwalks above.

"The HRT is federal law enforcement's first-tier tactical team because of its advanced training and capabilities," noted Special Agent Kevin Cornelius, a section chief and former operator who now commands the team. That's the main difference between SWAT teams and the HRT. Whereas Bureau SWAT members train a few days each month—while maintaining their full-time jobs as investigators—HRT operators train full-time and have capabilities SWAT teams don't possess, such as the ability to operate in extreme climates.

"When a crisis situation exceeds the capabilities of local and regional tactical teams," Cornelius said, "then the HRT gets the call. Because of our extensive training, we are more prepared to address complex problems."

After New Operator Training School, graduates join individual teams within the HRT. For the first year, they continue to develop their basic assault skills—but they must also specialize as breachers, communicators, or medics. The fast-paced culture is "very satisfying," Piser said, but it's not without sacrifice. Operators are often away from their families for extended periods and can be called away with little notice.

"The time away from home is difficult," said Sean Joyce, a former HRT member who is now the FBI's deputy director, "but that's something operators and families learn to cope with." He added that the extensive, continuous training HRT operators go through that keeps them from their personal lives is absolutely essential—"because what you do in practice is what you're going to do when the real game is on."

Part 4: Night maneuvers—tracking a terrorist (page 18)

Legal Attaché London
Then and Now

Seventy years ago this coming Monday, Arthur M. Thurston was officially named legal attaché of the U.S. Embassy in wartime London. Three months earlier, on November 16, 1942, he had, at the invitation of U.S. Ambassador John Winant, opened the office for liaison purposes in the 1 Grosvenor Square embassy. Now, as "legat," Thurston was already highly connected with his colleagues in MI-5 and MI-6.

It was a fearful time to be in London, but an enormously productive time as well. British intelligence had developed Ultra—which intercepted and later decoded radio and cable messages sent by the Nazis to their clandestine networks worldwide. Thurston was given access to the decrypted messages in January 1943 and, under the codename Ostrich, forwarded intelligence to FBI Headquarters that related to possible German espionage in the United States. Ultimately, Ostrich would crucially assist our mandated intelligence operations in South America, control movement of double agents, and penetrate German intelligence. Postwar, there would be critical legat assistance and liaison in the Klaus Fuchs exposé. Even by 1951, when the office was staffed with a single agent and two clerks, Legat John Cimperman was putting in 11-plus hour days and had 235 open cases that were pending resolution. Gamely, he described that time as "an unusually light period."

And so began the friendships and cooperative relationships between the FBI and British law enforcement and intelligence services that flourish to this day.

Today, Legat London is staffed with Legal Attaché Scott Cruse, a deputy and five assistant legats, an intelligence analyst, and four office administrators. And guess what? They are still putting in 11-plus hour days. It is an incredibly busy and intense office, thanks to a world in turmoil.

Yesteryear's threats of wartime and postwar espionage have given way to 21st century threats to national security—notably international terrorism, the FBI's top priority. And without the help of our international partners, we could not be successful.

Consider the recent extradition of five alleged terrorists from Mildenhall Royal Air Force Base in the U.K. on October 5, 2012. Following U.S. charges,

The FBI's legal attaché office in London was in the U.S. Embassy building at 1 Grosvenor Square.

all had been arrested by our British colleagues—one in 1998, one in 1999, and three in 2004. All fought extradition in the U.K. and, when that failed, all appealed to the European Court of Human Rights on the grounds that, among other things, U.S. sentences were too long. After they had exhausted all appeals, Legat London worked with the U.K.'s Crown Prosecution Service and the London Metropolitan Police Service's SO15 counterterrorism branch and extradition unit—not to mention with our U.S. military and federal partners—to coordinate the high-profile transport of Abu Hamza Al-Masri, Adel Abdel Bary, and Khalid Al-Fawwaz to New York City and Syed Talha Ahsan and Babar Ahmad to New Haven, Connecticut.

We thank our partners in the U.K. every single day for sharing information that protects both of our countries and brings terrorists and criminals to justice. Michael S. Welch, assistant director of our International Operations Division, says it well: "In today's era of asymmetrical threats, only the closest relationships among law enforcement and intelligence personnel and their most determined will to share intelligence can help all of us identify, disrupt, and prosecute international criminals and terrorists."

Edward J. Schwartz
United States Courthouse

EXIT

FBI

Left: An FBI agent at the scene of the 2008 bombing of a federal courthouse in San Diego.

Weapon of Mass Deception
Courthouse Bomber Receives 55-Year Sentence

When the bomb went off in the middle of the night at the San Diego federal courthouse in May 2008, the message seemed clear: This was an act of terror—or possibly revenge. At the time, no one would have guessed that the real motive was all about money.

The strange case of the courthouse bombing came to a close recently when the last defendant, Donny Love, Sr.—the mastermind of the operation—was sentenced to 55 years in prison for using a weapon of mass destruction and other charges.

Love persuaded his sometime girlfriend and two others who trusted him and depended on him for drugs to carry out the bombing. He then planned to contact authorities with information about the crime so he could collect a reward.

"The plot seems so odd and bizarre," said Special Agent Justin Zuccolotto, who investigated the case, "but you can begin to understand it when you understand Love's ability to control and manipulate the people around him. His actions showed that he was a predator who didn't care about anyone but himself."

The explosive device set in the entrance to the Edward J. Schwartz Federal Courthouse consisted of three powerful pipe bombs placed inside a backpack that was also filled with 110 roofing nails. When it exploded, the bomb blew out the courthouse doors and sent shrapnel and nails

flying in all directions—over a block away and at least six stories into the air.

Although no one was injured in the blast, "we were very lucky this wasn't a murder scene," Zuccolotto said. "There was no reason to put nails in the bomb; the bomb by itself would have been enough for his scheme."

After the explosion, there was an immediate response from local authorities and members of the FBI's San Diego Field Office, including the Bureau's Evidence Response Team and Joint Terrorism Task Force. Plenty of evidence was found at the scene, including surveillance video showing a person igniting the backpack.

A few days later, Love contacted the FBI through an attorney and said he would provide information about the crime in exchange for a $75,000 reward and leniency on criminal charges pending against him. He intended to provide false information, directly from him and from those he controlled.

"His actions were beyond callous," Zuccolotto said. "Thinking of anybody else's well being never crossed his mind. It was all about him making a buck or saving his skin."

Love, 44, who had worked for the local water department for a decade but had recently been fired, was behind on his mortgage payments. He thought the reward money would solve all his problems.

"He really thought he could get away with it," Zuccolotto said. But his story soon fell apart, and two of his accomplices—including his former girlfriend—later became cooperating witnesses in the case against him. Those two each received 10-year sentences, and another accomplice was sentenced to 11 years.

Zuccolotto credits local authorities; the Bureau of Alcohol, Tobacco, Firearms, and Explosives; the United States Attorney's Office; the FBI Laboratory; and local, state, and federal members of the Joint Terrorism Task Force for bringing the case to a successful conclusion. "Everybody worked well together," he said. "We needed to get this guy off the streets."

The Cyber Threat
Planning for the Way Ahead

Denial of service attacks, network intrusions, state-sponsored hackers bent on compromising our national security: The cyber threat is growing, and in response, said FBI Director Robert S. Mueller, the Bureau must continue to strengthen its partnerships with other government agencies and private industry—and take the fight to the criminals.

"Network intrusions pose urgent threats to our national security and to our economy," Mueller told a group of cyber security professionals in San Francisco today. "If we are to confront these threats successfully," he explained, "we must adopt a unified approach" that promotes partnerships and intelligence sharing—in the same way we responded to terrorism after the 9/11 attacks.

The FBI learned after 9/11 that "our mission was to use our skills and resources to identify terrorist threats and to find ways of disrupting those threats," Mueller said. "This has been the mindset at the heart of every terrorism investigation since then, and it must be true of every case in the cyber arena as well."

Partnerships that ensure the seamless flow of intelligence are critical in the fight against cyber crime, he explained. Within government, the National Cyber Investigative Joint Task Force, which comprises 19 separate agencies, serves as a focal point for cyber threat information. But private industry—a major victim of cyber intrusions—must also be "an essential partner," Mueller said, pointing to several successful initiatives.

The National Cyber Forensics and Training Alliance, for example, is a model for collaboration between private industry and law enforcement. The Pittsburgh-based organization includes more than 80 industry partners—from financial services, telecommunications, retail, and manufacturing, among other fields—who work with federal and international partners to provide real-time threat intelligence.

Another example is the Enduring Security Framework, a group that includes leaders from the private sector and the federal government who analyze current—and potential—threats related to denial of service attacks, malware, and emerging software and hardware vulnerabilities.

Director Mueller speaks to cyber security professionals in San Francisco.

Mueller also noted the Bureau's cyber outreach efforts to private industry. The Domestic Security Alliance Council, for instance, includes chief security officers from more than 200 companies, representing every critical infrastructure and business sector. InfraGard, an alliance between the FBI and industry, has grown from a single chapter in 1996 to 88 chapters today with nearly 55,000 members nationwide. And just last week, the FBI held the first session of the National Cyber Executive Institute, a three-day seminar to train leading industry executives on cyber threat awareness and information sharing.

"As noteworthy as these outreach programs may be, we must do more," Mueller said. **"We must build on these initiatives to expand the channels of information sharing and collaboration."**

He added, "For two decades, corporate cyber security has focused principally on reducing vulnerabilities. These are worthwhile efforts, but they cannot fully eliminate our vulnerabilities. We must identify and deter the persons behind those computer keyboards. And once we identify them—be they state actors, organized criminal groups, or 18-year-old hackers—we must devise a response that is effective, not just against that specific attack, but for all similar illegal activity."

"We need to abandon the belief that better defenses alone will be sufficient," Mueller said. "Instead of just building better defenses, we must build better relationships. If we do these things, and if we bring to these tasks the sense of urgency that this threat demands," he added, "I am confident that we can and will defeat cyber threats, now and in the years to come."

The Hostage Rescue Team
Part 4: An Exercise in Terror

The subject was overheard by a co-worker discussing five explosive devices he had secretly placed around the nation's capital. Intelligence suggested that the subject's laptop—which never left his side—was a triggering device that could be activated in a matter of seconds. The Hostage Rescue Team's mission: Capture the subject and secure his computer before he detonated the bombs.

The operation order was received at the HRT headquarters in Quantico, Virginia at 4:30 p.m., and the HRT Blue Operational Unit was assembled shortly thereafter. In less than two hours, they would deploy to the subject's farm in rural Virginia. Although everyone in the room knew this was a training exercise, the team was serious and attentive.

"We make these training scenarios as real as possible," said the HRT Blue Unit senior team leader. "This is how we maintain our skills." Tactical training operations are so realistic that scenarios are often drawn from real cases, and role players may change the scenario on the fly to force operators to think on their feet—just the way it happens on actual missions.

During the Blue Unit's initial briefing, operators were shown the subject's picture, along with aerial photos and topographical maps of the target location; they also received details about the subject's "pattern of life."

On a real mission, the team would rely on the support of intelligence analysts, communications experts, and others to get the job done. As part of the FBI's Critical Incident Response Group, the HRT also has other resources at its disposal, such as crisis negotiators.

Left: HRT operators using night-vision gear approach a suspect's home during a night-training exercise.

At the designated staging area, with the team's assaulters and snipers in full gear—including night-vision goggles to see in the dark—they walked with stealth through the woods and established a perimeter around the subject's residence (a vacant building loaned to the Bureau by a local sheriff's department). When they were all in place, the operation began.

The team had a solid plan for arresting the subject at his residence, but before the evening was over, operators would have to visit three different locations around the area to find and apprehend their target. Throughout the exercise, several wrinkles were thrown at the operators and each required a new contingency plan and significant coordination among the team.

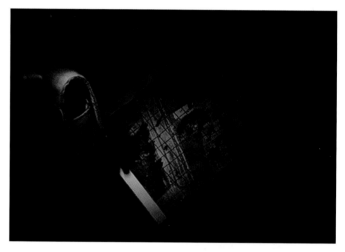

An HRT operator consults a map during a training exercise.

"As we get new intelligence, the operation plan changes and the team adapts," one team leader said. "In a real-world situation, you have to make decisions quickly—and usually under difficult circumstances."

That's why when HRT operators are not in mission status, they train constantly in the core areas of tactics, firearms, and physical fitness while waiting to deploy. For the HRT Blue Unit, this exercise was just another day at the office.

By 11 p.m., with the mission accomplished, the team was conducting an after-action briefing about what worked in tonight's operation and what could be improved. In a few minutes, they would head back to Quantico and stow their gear—until tomorrow.

Part 5: Held to a higher standard (page 19)

The Hostage Rescue Team
Part 5: Held to a Higher Standard

Jaime Atherton was a 30-year-old former Marine and Vietnam veteran when he became an FBI agent in 1976. He joined the SWAT team in our San Francisco office, and later, after a transfer to the FBI Laboratory's explosives unit in Quantico, Virginia, he heard about a brand new team that was forming—the Hostage Rescue Team.

The 1984 Summer Olympics in Los Angeles were approaching, and the federal government realized it needed a non-military counterterrorism tactical team to help safeguard the games—and to prevent a tragedy like the one that occurred at the Munich Olympics in 1972, when Palestinian gunmen took 11 Israeli athletes hostage and later murdered them. The responsibility for that new tactical team was given to the FBI, and Atherton (now retired) wanted to be a part of it.

"It appealed to me," he said, "the challenge that was involved, the chance to be a part of something new, and the ability to make a difference—that's why I joined the Bureau."

Atherton's bomb tech background in the Marines and the FBI made him well-suited for a new explosive breaching capability the HRT wanted to use, but first he had to survive the selection process, an arduous physical and mental test that was like nothing he had ever experienced.

For one thing, candidates didn't know what stressful endurance test or mental challenge was coming next. And they received no feedback on how they were doing. "You had no idea what the standards were or how you were being judged," he recalled. "That played on your mind."

Even after he made the team, becoming one of the Bureau's 50 first-generation HRT operators, no one was certain the concept of a full-time tactical team would succeed. "You've got to remember that in 1983 when it started, there were a lot of people who said, 'As soon as the Olympics are over, you guys are going to be reassigned.'"

HRT operators participate in an urban assault training exercise.

Three decades later, the team has proven its worth during hundreds of high-risk missions in every corner of the world—from the 1998 U.S. Embassy bombings in East Africa to deployments in Iraq and Afghanistan and the arrests of Top Ten fugitives and the D.C. snipers. They have achieved that success—through 27 generations of operators—because of the HRT's rigorous selection process and the individuals who have what it takes to make the team.

"We were always aware that we were being held to a higher standard, both professionally and personally," said Atherton, who spent 16 years as an operator and another decade working in the HRT program. "It's no different for today's operators."

Going back to that first selection, Atherton recalled, "When you saw the caliber of person that was there with you, the dedication that each of them had, you just wanted to do that much better yourself. If you scratch the surface of anyone who has ever been on the team," he added, "you are going to find the same personality traits and the same qualities and motivations."

Part 6: A harrowing mission in the Gulf of Aden (page 25)

Organized Retail Theft
Major Middle Eastern Crime Ring Dismantled

When it comes to shoplifting, this was a serious and sophisticated operation.

It involved members of a criminal group waltzing into major U.S. retail stores and pharmacies and brazenly walking out with stolen products of all kinds, from medicine and baby formula to health and beauty supplies. Those products were then repackaged and sold at rock bottom prices to various wholesalers, who, in some cases, sold them right back to the companies they had been stolen from.

The criminal bottom line: An estimated $10 million worth of products were swiped every year from 2008 to 2012. To make matters worse, many of the goods—some possibly compromised by being stored and shipped under improper conditions and some sold past their expiration dates—eventually ended up in the hands of an unsuspecting public.

It all came to an end thanks to a multi-agency investigation by the FBI, the Houston Police Department, and the Harris County Sheriff's Office, with the help of victim merchants. Earlier this month, one of the highest-ranking and most prolific fences in this Middle Eastern crime ring was convicted in federal court. Charges against other group members are pending.

Sameh Khaled Danhach, a native of Lebanon and a legal permanent resident of the U.S., headed up SKD Trading, Inc. and Lifetime Wholesale, Inc., both shell companies located in Houston that allowed Danhach and his conspirators to carry out their illegal activities.

The scheme. Danhach and others recruited "boosters"—individuals who lifted the merchandise from pharmacies and retailers—from among undocumented Mexican, Central American, and South American aliens in the United States. Booster crews traveled around Texas and other states and hit various businesses, often in cars rented by Danhach or his associates. For their efforts, they'd receive a small percentage of the actual value of the stolen property…always in cash so there would be no paper trail.

The boosters then shipped the merchandise back to Danhach's Houston warehouse using phony accounts with bogus business names, e-mail addresses, and credit cards set up by Danhach and others. These shipping companies were also victimized—they rarely, if ever, got paid.

The boosters shipped the stolen goods in case they were ever pulled over by law enforcement during routine traffic stops while they were driving back to Texas (that happened once, and Danhach wanted to make sure it never happened again).

Once the stolen merchandise was in Danhach's possession, he would have his people remove anti-theft devices and store stickers, and then he would once again—using phony business accounts—ship the goods to various wholesalers, who would put the stolen goods back into circulation.

In March 2012, a search warrant for Danhach's Houston warehouse turned up many interesting items: among them, more than $300,000 worth of stolen over-the-counter medications, shampoos, and baby formula, along with financial ledgers showing that from August 2011 to January 2012 alone, Danhach paid $1.8 million for stolen merchandise and sold it for $2.8 million for a net profit of $1 million.

Industry experts say organized retail crimes like this cost the U.S. about $30 billion a year. While that estimate includes other crimes like credit card fraud, gift card fraud, and price tag switching, the FBI generally focuses on the most significant retail theft cases involving the interstate transportation of stolen property.

New Top Ten Fugitive
Help Us Find a Murderer

Edwin Ernesto Rivera Gracias, wanted for the murder of a 69-year-old Colorado man who was dumped on the side of the road after being brutally beaten and stabbed, has been named to the Ten Most Wanted Fugitives list.

A reward of up to $100,000 is being offered for information leading directly to the arrest of Rivera Gracias, who is a member of the violent Mara Salvatrucha gang—MS-13—and is believed to be in El Salvador.

"Today we are asking for media and public assistance in bringing this dangerous fugitive to justice," said James Yacone, special agent in charge of our Denver Field Office.

Special Agent Phil Niedringhaus, who leads the FBI's violent crimes squad in Denver, noted, "MS-13 is one of the most violent gangs in the United States, and Rivera Gracias appears to have embraced that lifestyle."

The fugitive, a Salvadoran national, is approximately 29 to 33 years old with brown hair and brown eyes. He is 5'10" tall, weighs about 170 pounds, and has a variety of tattoos, including "MS-13" across his back, "LA" on his right forearm, and "Nena" on his left hand.

The murder he is charged with occurred in August 2011. The victim—a long-time family acquaintance of Rivera Gracias' teenage girlfriend—was choked, beaten, and stabbed. His body was then dumped in the mountains outside of Denver, where it was later discovered by a bicyclist.

The investigation soon focused on Rivera Gracias and accomplices, including his girlfriend, explained Special Agent Russ Humphrey, a member of the FBI's Rocky Mountain Safe Streets Task Force, who worked the case. "The murder was vicious," Humphrey said.

Rivera Gracias fled from Denver to Los Angeles and is now believed to be in his native El Salvador. Intelligence analysts with our MS-13 National Gang Task Force helped to positively identify Rivera Gracias, who also goes by the names Ernest Rivera and Edwin Rivera.

Rivera Gracias has ties to other MS-13 gang members in Colorado, Los Angeles, and El Salvador and may attempt to gain entry to the U.S. using fraudulent identification. He may also visit Mexico and Guatemala.

FBI TEN MOST WANTED FUGITIVE

Unlawful Flight to Avoid Prosecution - First Degree Murder

EDWIN ERNESTO RIVERA GRACIAS

"Elevating Rivera Gracias to the Top Ten list sends a message," said Special Agent Niedringhaus. "No matter where you are as a fugitive—in the U.S. or anywhere in the world—we are coming after you."

He added, "The FBI has put significant resources into fighting MS-13, and our gang task force works closely with our international partners to gather intelligence to help dismantle this transnational group. I think our chances of catching Rivera Gracias are excellent, especially with the substantial reward being offered."

We need your help: If you have any information concerning the whereabouts of Rivera Gracias, please contact the FBI's Denver Field Office at 303-629-7171 or your nearest law enforcement agency or U.S. Embassy or Consulate. You can also submit a tip online.

Since its creation in 1950—63 years ago today—498 fugitives have been on the Ten Most Wanted Fugitives list and 467 have been apprehended or located, 154 of them as a result of citizen cooperation.

03/27/13 Update: Edwin Ernesto Rivera Gracias was taken into custody in El Salvador and transferred to authorities in Denver, Colorado.

Left: Cartha "Deke" DeLoach, center, joins FBI Director J. Edgar Hoover and Roy Moore, special agent in charge of the Jackson Field Office, during a ceremony in Jackson, Mississippi on July 10, 1964.

Remembering 'Deke' DeLoach
Trusted Adviser to J. Edgar Hoover Dies at 92

Special Agent Cartha "Deke" DeLoach, a trusted adviser to FBI Director J. Edgar Hoover who oversaw the investigation into the assassination of Dr. Martin Luther King, Jr. and served as the Bureau's liaison to President Lyndon B. Johnson after John F. Kennedy's assassination in 1963, died Wednesday evening in South Carolina. He was 92.

The former assistant to the Director, who was third in command at the FBI—after Hoover and Associate Director Clyde Tolson—until retiring in 1970, joined the Bureau as a clerk in August 1942 in what was then the Identification Division. Four months later, he became a special agent. Over the course of his career, he worked in the Norfolk and Cleveland Field Offices. He also held a number of leadership positions at Headquarters, including assistant director of the Crime Records Division from 1959 to 1965, where he pushed to establish the National Crime Information Center, or NCIC, which launched in 1967. His tenure at the FBI saw major shifts in the Bureau's priorities, from preventing saboteurs and espionage during World War II to battling the Ku Klux Klan in the late 50s and early 60s to investigating major civil rights cases.

"Deke's commitment to the FBI and to the American people at large was a hallmark of his life," FBI Director Robert S. Mueller said in a statement. "We will remember him as a dedicated special agent and a committed public servant—one who upheld the highest ideals of the FBI."

Indeed, it was DeLoach who in 1963 served as the Bureau's link to President Lyndon Johnson's White House after the Kennedy assassination. In 1964, when three civil rights workers went missing in Mississippi, the president called him almost daily for case updates. It was DeLoach who personally called Johnson to tell him the bodies had been found. In an oral history recorded in 1991, DeLoach recalled traveling down to Mississippi with Hoover and Tolson and experiencing firsthand the challenging climate facing investigators.

"FBI agents were shouldered off the sidewalk, refused food in restaurants, a Klansman put rattlesnakes down on the floor of the driver's seat of an agent's car," DeLoach recalled. "The FBI took a lot of abuse; they worked ungodly amounts of overtime. I was with them down there part of the time; I know."

DeLoach was the last of the FBI's senior leaders from the turbulent civil rights era. He was a principal supervisor in the investigation of the murdered civil rights workers—the Mississippi Burning case. He also supervised the hunt for James Earl Ray after Ray killed Dr. King in 1968.

"The FBI was involved at the very center of the civil rights struggle," said FBI Historian Dr. John Fox, "and Deke DeLoach was at the very center of the FBI."

In an interview last June with the Center for Intelligence and Security Studies, DeLoach said the FBI helped turn the tide against the Klan and its followers. "Eventually I think the good work of the FBI and the Department of Justice…caused the sympathizers' beliefs to wane and recognize this is not a good way of life," DeLoach said.

DeLoach served the FBI for 28 years—the last five as a key adviser to Hoover. After retiring, he went to work for private industry and in 1995 wrote a book titled *Hoover's FBI: The Inside Story by Hoover's Trusted Lieutenant.* A longtime resident of Hilton Head Island, South Carolina, DeLoach received the state's highest civilian honor for his years of service to the town and his home state.

The Gardner Museum Theft
Reward Offered for Return of Artwork

Today, the FBI—along with Boston's Isabella Stewart Gardner Museum and the U.S. Attorney's Office in Massachusetts—asked for the public's help in recovering artwork stolen from the museum more than two decades ago in what remains the largest property crime in U.S. history.

At a press conference this afternoon in Boston on the 23rd anniversary of the theft, officials hoped to get the attention of those who might have or know the whereabouts of the 13 stolen works of art—including rare paintings by Rembrandt and Vermeer—by publicly restating a $5 million reward.

"Today, we are pleased to announce that the FBI has made significant investigative progress in the search for the stolen art from the Isabella Stewart Gardner Museum," said Richard DesLauriers, special agent in charge of the FBI's Boston Field Office. "We've determined in the years after the theft that the art was transported to the Connecticut and Philadelphia regions. But we haven't identified where the art is right now, and that's why we are asking the public for help."

"With these considerable developments in the investigation over the last couple of years," said Special Agent Geoff Kelly, who heads the FBI investigation, "it's likely over time someone has seen the art hanging on a wall, placed above a mantel, or stored in an attic. We want that person to call the FBI."

Anthony Amore, the Gardner Museum's chief of security, explained that the museum is offering a $5 million reward "for information that leads directly to the recovery of all of our items in good condition. What that means is that you don't have to hand us the paintings to be eligible for the reward." Amore added, "We hope that through this type of public campaign, people will see how earnest we are in our attempts to pay this reward and make our institution whole."

Officials stressed that anyone with information about the artwork can contact the FBI, the museum, or the U.S. Attorney's Office directly or through a third party. "An individual who wishes to protect his or her identity can go through an attorney and the reward can be paid through

An empty frame in the Dutch Room of the Gardner Museum, where Rembrandt's *The Storm on the Sea of Galilee* and *A Lady and Gentleman in Black* once hung.

an attorney," Amore said. "There is no shortage of ways to get information to us. We simply want to recover our paintings and move forward. This is the 23rd anniversary of the robbery," he said. "It's time for these paintings to come home."

We need your help: If you have information about the missing Gardner Museum artwork, you can contact the FBI's hotline at 1-800-CALL-FBI or submit a tip on our website. All information will be held in the strictest confidence.

Scan this QR code with your smartphone to access related videos and photos, or visit www.fbi.gov/gardner.

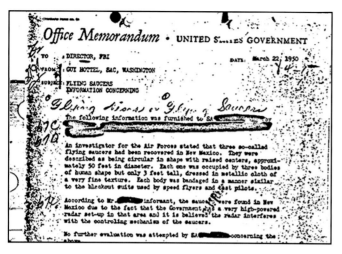

Left: A single-page March 22, 1950 memo by Guy Hottel, special agent in charge of the Washington Field Office, regarding UFOs is the most viewed document in the FBI Vault, our online repository of public records.

UFOs or No?
The Guy Hottel Memo

It's the most popular file in the FBI Vault—our high-tech electronic reading room housing various Bureau records released under the Freedom of Information Act. Over the past two years, this file has been viewed nearly a million times. Yet, it is only a single page, relaying an unconfirmed report that the FBI never even followed up on.

The file in question is a memo dated March 22, 1950—63 years ago last week. It was authored by Guy Hottel, then head of our field office in Washington, D.C. Like all memos to FBI Headquarters at that time, it was addressed to Director J. Edgar Hoover and recorded and indexed in FBI records.

The subject of the memo was anything but ordinary. It related a story told to one of our agents by a third party who said an Air Force investigator had reported that three "flying saucers" were recovered in New Mexico. The memo provided the following detail:

> "They [the saucers] were described as being circular in shape with raised centers, approximately 50 feet in diameter. Each one was occupied by three bodies of human shape but only three feet tall, dressed in metallic cloth of a very fine texture. Each body was bandaged in a manner similar to the blackout suits used by speed fliers and test pilots."

After relaying an informant's claim that the saucers had been found because the government's "high-powered radar" in the area had interfered with "the controlling mechanism of the saucers," the memo ends simply by saying that "[n]o further evaluation was attempted" concerning the matter by the FBI agent.

That might have been the end of this particular story, just another informational dead end in the FBI files. But when we launched the Vault in April 2011, some media outlets noticed the Hottel memo and erroneously reported that the FBI had posted proof of a UFO crash at Roswell, New Mexico and the recovery of wreckage and alien corpses. The resulting stories went viral, and traffic to the new Vault soared.

So what's the real story? A few facts to keep in mind:

First, the Hottel memo isn't new. It was first released publicly in the late 1970s and had been posted on the FBI website for several years prior to the launch of the Vault.

Second, the Hottel memo is dated nearly three years after the infamous events in Roswell in July 1947. There is no reason to believe the two are connected. The FBI file on Roswell (another popular page) is posted elsewhere on the Vault.

Third, as noted in an earlier story, the FBI has only occasionally been involved in investigating reports of UFOs and extraterrestrials. For a few years after the Roswell incident, Director Hoover did order his agents—at the request of the Air Force—to verify any UFO sightings. That practice ended in July 1950, four months *after* the Hottel memo, suggesting that our Washington Field Office didn't think enough of that flying saucer story to look into it.

Finally, the Hottel memo does not prove the existence of UFOs; it is simply a second- or third-hand claim that we never investigated. Some people believe the memo repeats a hoax that was circulating at that time, but the Bureau's files have no information to verify that theory.

Sorry, no smoking gun on UFOs. The mystery remains…

The Hostage Rescue Team
Part 6: Mission in the Gulf of Aden

Early one morning in Nairobi, Kenya, information began flowing into the FBI's legal attaché office there concerning the hijacking of a private yacht with four American passengers on board in the Gulf of Aden—perhaps the most pirated body of water in the world.

A Hostage Rescue Team operator temporarily stationed in Nairobi mobilized immediately—within hours, he was on his way to the scene off the coast of Somalia. Simultaneously, a crisis negotiator and former HRT operator was dispatched to a Navy destroyer that was shadowing the hijacked S/V *Quest*.

Events that unfolded over the next days were tragic—the Americans aboard the 54-foot pleasure boat were murdered by the armed Somali pirates—but the work of the HRT operators and other FBI agents helped make certain that those responsible for the crime were brought to justice, including a Somali co-conspirator who was not among the 19 hijackers on the vessel.

The case serves as a sobering reminder of the value HRT operators and other FBI personnel add to U.S. military and international law enforcement missions around the globe in the fight against crime and terrorism.

"HRT operators possess the tactical skills that allow them to integrate with entities like the Department of Defense when there is a crime scene in a non-permissive environment," explained one of the operators who responded to the *Quest* hijacking in February 2011. "But they are also experienced investigators. Having an FBI agent on the scene was a huge benefit," he added, "because it allowed us to protect the integrity of the crime scene, to collect evidence, and to present that evidence in court."

The pirates were attempting to sail the *Quest* and the hostages back to Somalia when they were overtaken by Navy warships. Military negotiators tried to secure the hostages' release, but, according to court documents, the pirates said they would not comply. Some of the pirates began discussing killing hostages to get the U.S. boats to retreat. A rocket-propelled grenade was launched against a Navy ship as a warning shot. At the same time, hijackers guarding the hostages began firing their weapons.

Satellite view of Somalia and the Indian Ocean. The Gulf of Aden and Yemen are seen to the north.

Seeing small-arms fire erupting from the cabin of the *Quest*, Navy personnel immediately launched an emergency assault against the pirates, but it was too late for the hostages.

An HRT operator followed the initial assault team and helped secure the yacht and detain the surviving pirates. Later, our agents began to process the crime scene.

"It was standard FBI crime-scene processing," the HRT operator explained. "We began photographing and logging evidence, and we were able to provide a substantial amount of material to our New York Evidence Response Team when they arrived later in Djibouti, where the *Quest* had been towed."

That evidence would be significant in federal court in Norfolk, Virginia, where multiple Somali pirates have since pled guilty to piracy and murder and received life terms in U.S. prison.

"That outcome was extremely gratifying," the HRT operator said of the hijackers' sentences. "In a difficult environment, we were able to do what agents are supposed to do, which is to bring criminals to justice."

Can You Crack a Code?
Try Your Hand at Cryptanalysis

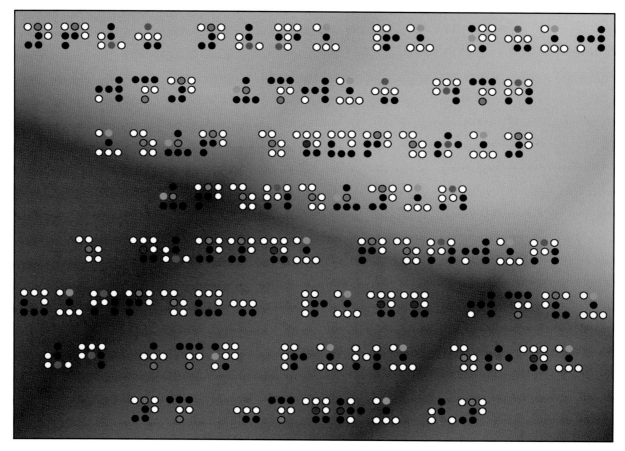

The cryptanalysts in our FBI Laboratory are pros at code-cracking…but it has been a few years since we have challenged you to give it a go.

We've done it a bit differently this time around, creating our first dot code. Good luck!

To learn more about the types of ciphers and codes that terrorists, spies, and criminals use to conceal their communications, see the article "Analysis of Criminal Codes and Ciphers" from our Forensic Science Communications publication. You can also read about famous cases over the years in the article, "Code Breaking in Law Enforcement: A 400-Year History."

To see the answer, visit www.fbi.gov/crackthecode.

The Best and Brightest
FBI Presents Director's Community Leadership Awards

Throughout the year, dedicated and selfless individuals and organizations make extraordinary contributions to their communities across the United States. And every year, the FBI honors the very best among them with its Director's Community Leadership Award.

Each FBI field office selects one individual or organization for the award, and each award recipient is publicly recognized at the local level. At a later date, all winners are brought to FBI Headquarters to be presented with their award by the FBI Director. And that's just what happened today, when the nearly 60 Director's Community Leadership Award recipients from 2012 were presented with their award by Director Robert Mueller during a ceremony in Washington, D.C.

The award recipients come from different backgrounds, different professional fields, and different parts of the country, and the issues they choose to focus on vary greatly. But they all have the same motivation—a desire to reach out to those in need and make their communities a safer place to live.

Speaking to the honorees at today's ceremony, Director Mueller said, "You [all] share the same vision for our nation's future—one of hope, peace, and justice. You also share a willingness to lead—a willingness to step up and step forward—when countless others instead choose to take a back seat."

Here are just a few examples of how one individual or organization can make a difference:

- In Atlanta, **Soumaya Khalifa** founded the Islamic Speakers Bureau to educate those unfamiliar with the Islamic faith and provide insight into how Muslim Americans live their daily lives. She often presents training to students, business executives, and military and law enforcement personnel.

- In Birmingham, the non-profit **Prescott House**, a children's advocacy center, works with federal, state, and local law enforcement to conduct forensic interviews of children who may have witnessed a violent crime or been the victim of sexual abuse, child pornography, or severe neglect.

- In Buffalo, **Nestor Hernandez** is the former director of the Belle Center, a community center in a

predominantly Hispanic neighborhood known for gang activity. The center provides a safe place for children to play, teaches English to adult immigrants, and offers affordable day care for working parents.

- In Memphis, **Julaine Harris**, while working for corporate and non-profit organizations, has spent years advocating programs that focus on reducing gang activities, protecting children from domestic violence, and providing affordable housing for low-income families.

- In Minneapolis, **Ka Joog**—a Somali American youth organization—encourages young people to stay away from illegal drugs, violence, radicalization, and other negative influences while learning to assimilate into American society. The group also hosts regular seminars with members of the community and law enforcement.

- In San Juan, **Basta Ya Puerto Rico** is an anti-violence non-profit organization. Among its accomplishments, the group created an application for smart phones that helps citizens report crime to police and developed "safety zone" areas with the combined resources of government, business, and community.

- In Washington, D.C., **Humera Khan**, a dedicated advocate for American Muslims, is the founder of Mueflehun, a research organization that promotes service-minded communities and justice. Khan's organization offers recommendations to multiple government agencies about countering homegrown terrorism and violent extremism.

Congratulations to all of our award recipients, who we hope will inspire a brand new generation of community leaders.

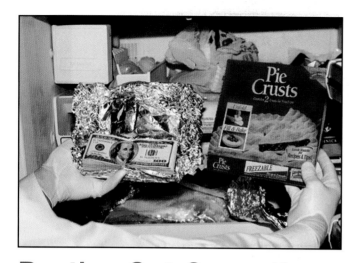

Left: Part of the $90,000 found in then-Congressman William Jefferson's freezer during a law enforcement search of his residence; this particular bundle was wrapped in aluminum foil and concealed inside a pie crust box.

Rooting Out Corruption
A Look Back at the Jefferson Case

It's our job to follow the evidence, wherever it might lead. That's certainly true in cases of public corruption, our highest priority among criminal threats.

So back in 2005, when we received reliable information that a sitting member of the U.S. Congress was allegedly using his official position to solicit bribes from American companies interested in doing business in Africa, we opened an investigation.

The congressman in question was William J. Jefferson, who had been serving Louisiana's 2nd congressional district since 1991.

Our investigation revealed that from 2000 to 2005, Jefferson sought hundreds of millions of dollars for himself and other co-conspirators from companies whose success depended on the approval of certain U.S. and West African government agencies. He ended up pocketing more than $478,000, but Jefferson wasted significantly more in U.S. government resources to further his illegal aims.

At one point, Jefferson turned from bribe recipient to bribe payer when he was caught on camera taking $100,000 in cash from our cooperating witness for use in paying off an African government official. A few days later, the FBI—while serving a search warrant on his residence—found $90,000 of that same cash in Jefferson's freezer. And a legally authorized search of Jefferson's office turned up documents later used as evidence during his trial.

Our investigation uncovered at least 11 distinct bribery schemes that involved Jefferson leading official business delegations to Africa, corresponding with U.S. and foreign government officials on congressional letterhead, and using some of his own staffers—unbeknownst to them—to promote the bribe-paying businesses.

In addition to damaging recorded conversations between Jefferson and our cooperating witness, his trial also featured more than 45 witnesses, including a dozen U.S. government officials he tried to influence to get favorable treatment for the businesses promising him bribes. He was convicted in August 2009 and ultimately sentenced to 13 years in prison. Jefferson appealed several times, but last November, the U.S. Supreme Court denied his petition to review his conviction.

Like many of our corruption cases, our investigation of Jefferson involved the use of sophisticated techniques like cooperating witnesses, consensual monitoring, court-authorized electronic surveillance, video surveillance, and analysis of financial records…all capabilities we've used against organized crime, sophisticated financial fraud rings, international drug cartels, and more. Because of our experience, our tools and techniques, our resources and reach, and our ability and authority, the FBI has a singular charge to investigate and root out corruption at all levels of government.

FBI Agent Tim Thibault, who worked the case out of our Washington Field Office, stressed the importance of a cooperating witness—a Virginia businesswoman—in the investigation: "She came to us saying that Congressman Jefferson offered to use his congressional office to assist her company in an international business deal in exchange for a percentage ownership of her company. She agreed to cooperate by providing us with historical information regarding her interactions with the congressman and other co-conspirators and by wearing a body recorder and meeting with the congressman to help the FBI gather valuable evidence of his corrupt activity."

You can help. If you suspect public corruption at any level, please submit an online tip or call one of the FBI's public corruption hotlines.

FBI Gun Collection
Firearms That Help Solve Crimes

If every gun tells a story, the FBI's reference firearms collection could fill a very, very large book. The inventory of more than 7,000 firearms—curated over 80 years—contains just about every make and model, from John Dillinger's Prohibition-era revolver to the modern battlefield's M16 and almost everything in between.

Housed at the FBI Laboratory in Quantico, Virginia, the racks of weapons are not a musty exhibit of museum pieces, though some rare items would certainly qualify. Rather, the ever-expanding collection is a hands-on reference catalog for the Lab's firearms examiners to study, take apart, reassemble, and test fire to support investigations. By maintaining a working library of virtually every handgun and rifle—along with a database of their unique toolmarks—examiners are able to identify and substantiate for investigators what weapons may have been used in criminal acts.

"Oftentimes, this collection is used in active cases in comparing known samples from our collection with question samples from the field," said John Webb, a firearms examiner in the Lab's Firearms/Toolmarks Unit. "Often, an investigator will receive a part of a firearm or a firearm that isn't functional. We can take that and compare it with our reference collection, determine what isn't functioning, and repair it so we can obtain the test fires we need to conduct examinations with bullets and cartridge cases."

Most of the firearms come from closed investigations, though some are purchased and still others arrive as donations. In most closed cases, guns that were held as evidence in court are sent back to the Lab, where examiners can add them to the reference collection (whole or in parts) or have them destroyed. By continuously adding new pieces to the collection, the FBI aims to have a duplicate of every firearm. Sometimes a case could hinge on linking a firearm component to a similar part on a reference gun.

"The collection has been extremely useful in criminal cases, not only for an examiner's experience and education in handling nearly every firearm case that comes into the Laboratory," said Webb, "but it has been directly responsible for assisting to solve crimes."

The collection goes beyond firearms and includes accessories like suppressors, magazines, and muzzle

The reference firearms collection includes one of gangster "Pretty Boy" Floyd's Colt Model 1911 pistols.

attachments, as well as grenade and rocket launchers. Another reference collection, the standard ammunition file, catalogs more than 15,000 types of commercial and military ammunition.

While the breadth of the firearms collection is noteworthy, the historic provenance of some of the weapons shows it's a truly unique cache. Here you will find John Dillinger's .45-caliber revolver, Ma Barker and her gang's arsenal, and "Pretty Boy" Floyd's Colt Model 1911. There's an old Thompson submachine gun concealed in a guitar case, and a pistol hidden in the cut pages of a rare first edition of *Gone with the Wind*.

These aren't the most important weapons in the collection, however. Examiners will tell you the single most important piece—in a collection that spans more than a century of firearms history and ingenuity—is the one that helps investigators close a case on any given day. The same philosophy has informed the Lab's meticulous stewardship of the collection for eight decades.

"We are only a small part of this collection," Webb said. "It was here long before I was, and it will be here long after I'm gone."

Scan this QR code with your smartphone to access related video and photos, or visit www.fbi.gov/guncollection.

Insider Threat
Soldier Receives 16-Year Sentence for Attempted Espionage

A 22-year-old military police officer in Alaska has been sentenced to a 16-year jail term in connection with his efforts to sell classified documents to a person he believed was a Russian intelligence officer.

In 2011, William Millay was stationed at Joint Base Elmendorf-Richardson near Anchorage when he began to talk to—and solicit help from—other military members regarding selling classified national defense information to the Russians.

"This case really drives home the point that the insider threat is alive and well," said Special Agent Sam Johnson, who supervises a national security squad in our Anchorage Division. "That's why counterintelligence investigations continue to be a very high priority for the FBI."

Millay, who joined the Army in 2007 and had served a combat tour in Iraq, was known to have harsh and sometimes radical views of the military and the U.S. government—the white supremacist tattoos on his body likely reflect his ideology. But his attempt at spying had nothing to do with ideology or politics, Johnson said. Instead, he was motivated by greed.

"Money was what he was after," Johnson explained. "He was willing to sell sensitive information—to potentially endanger his fellow military members as well as the security of the country—for a payday."

The Russian officer he believed he was dealing with, however, was really an FBI undercover operative. The case played out like a spy thriller, with Millay placing secret documents about military technology at a dead drop site—a pre-arranged hiding place—and later retrieving a payment of $3,000 in exchange.

After an extensive investigation, Millay was arrested in October 2011; in addition to attempted espionage, he was charged with soliciting another individual to commit espionage. He pled guilty to these and other violations of the Uniform Code of Military Justice at a military court proceeding in March and was sentenced by a panel of military members earlier this month.

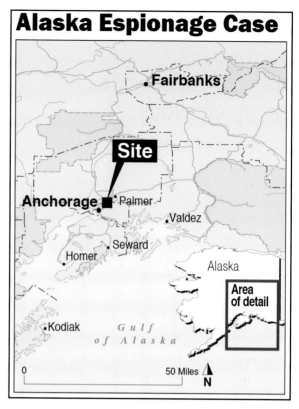

Alaska Espionage Case

The investigation revealed that Millay had approached several soldiers about his treasonous plan, said Special Agent Derrick Criswell, who worked the case. "Some of the individuals he made statements to did not take him seriously," Criswell noted, "but some did. Still, no one came forward to report his activity."

Both Criswell and Johnson believe the fact that no one reported Millay further illustrates the need to raise awareness about the insider threat and the risk it poses to national security. "One person can do a tremendous amount of damage," Johnson said.

Criswell's duties as a counterintelligence investigator include presenting briefings to government and industry organizations regarding espionage and the insider threat. Despite his familiarity with the problem, though, Criswell added, "It is still shocking and always disappointing to identify anyone who is willing to betray his country in this manner."

The Bureau investigated the case jointly with Army Counterintelligence and the Air Force Office of Special Investigations. "This has been a significant case for Alaska," Johnson said, adding, "It's the first known espionage arrest and prosecution that I am aware of in the state. And if it can happen here, it can happen anywhere."

A Different Kind of Outreach

Evidence Response Teams Connect with Kids

Members of our Evidence Response Teams (ERTs)—located in FBI offices around the country—often spend their days at scenes of deadly crimes or mass disaster sites collecting evidence to determine what happened and identify criminals or victims.

But once in a while—as their hectic schedules allow—our ERT personnel leave behind the grim nature of their jobs to take part in outreach efforts with young people in their communities, demonstrating forensic procedures and often inspiring their audiences to consider a scientific or other type of career in the FBI.

Over the past couple of years, ERT members have taken part in about 500 community events around the country—usually through the Bureau's community outreach program—and have reached an untold number of youngsters, from kindergartners to college students. These events include school career days and forensics classes; law school presentations; activities sponsored by youth groups, leadership groups, ethnic community-based groups, other law enforcement agencies, and businesses; summer camps; museum programs; county and state fairs; and police academies.

The forensic procedures most often demonstrated? Using alternate light sources—like ultraviolet—to recover virtually invisible evidence, dusting for fingerprints, casting shoe and tire print impressions, sketching crime scenes, and recovering hair and fiber evidence. Another big draw is a tour of the ERT crime scene truck.

Members of our ERT staff who take part in these events believe in their value, both for the students who participate and for the FBI. Here's what a few of them had to say about their experiences:

"We were invited to speak at a forensics class at a high school but ended up addressing the entire school. We set up demonstrations, allowing the students to see some of our evidence collection techniques first-hand. They saw how similar and how different evidence collection is when compared to what's on television."
- **ERT member, Charlotte**

A member of the Charlotte ERT demonstrates some evidence collection techniques at a local high school.

"Our presentations almost always include a discussion of the ERT's 12-step process to manage a crime scene, followed by a show-and-tell of several pieces of ERT equipment and supplies. A common theme at all of these events is that the kids see us as real people. And because some of the youngest kids we meet sometimes don't seem to grasp what we do, I usually bring a football or baseball to toss around at the outdoor events—plenty of smiles in return!"
- **ERT member, Cleveland**

"Among other activities, we take part annually in Kids and Cops Day at the Texas State Fair. We prepare an ERT display and let kids lift their own fingerprints off the side of an ERT response vehicle. The feedback we get is always positive, and the event is also very rewarding—many people stop by the booth just to thank us for what we do."
- **ERT member, Dallas**

Special Agent Dayna Sepeck is chief of the Evidence Response Team Unit at the FBI Laboratory. She strongly believes in the value of these interactions between ERT personnel and young people. "By meeting with these kids one on one, school by school, community by community, we hope to get them thinking about working at the FBI when they're older. We also hope that, as adults looking back on their interaction with us, they'll be fully supportive of our mission to protect the nation."

New Most Wanted Terrorist

Joanne Chesimard First Woman Added to List

On the 40th anniversary of the cold-blooded murder of a New Jersey state trooper, the fugitive convicted of the killing, Joanne Chesimard, has been named a Most Wanted Terrorist by the FBI—the first woman ever to make the list.

Officials from the FBI and the New Jersey State Police made the announcement this morning during a press conference, noting that the FBI is offering a reward of up to $1 million for information leading to the apprehension of Chesimard, who is believed to be living in Cuba under political asylum. Additionally, the state of New Jersey is offering an independent reward of up to $1 million, bringing the total maximum reward to $2 million.

"Joanne Chesimard is a domestic terrorist who murdered a law enforcement officer execution-style," said Aaron Ford, special agent in charge of our Newark Division. "Today, on the anniversary of Trooper Werner Foerster's death, we want the public to know that we will not rest until this fugitive is brought to justice."

"This case is just as important today as it was when it happened 40 years ago," added Mike Rinaldi, a lieutenant in the New Jersey State Police and member of our Joint Terrorism Task Force (JTTF) in Newark. "Bringing Joanne Chesimard back here to face justice is still a top priority," he said.

On May 2, 1973, Chesimard and a pair of accomplices were stopped by two troopers for a motor vehicle violation on the New Jersey Turnpike. At the time, Chesimard—a member of the violent revolutionary activist organization known as the Black Liberation Army—was wanted for her involvement in several felonies, including bank robbery.

Chesimard and her accomplices opened fire on the troopers. One officer was wounded, and his partner—Trooper Foerster—was shot and killed at point-blank range. One of Chesimard's accomplices was killed in the shootout and the other was arrested and remains in jail.

Chesimard fled but was apprehended. In 1977, she was found guilty of first-degree murder, armed robbery, and other crimes and was sentenced to life in prison. Less than two years later, she escaped from prison and lived underground before surfacing in Cuba in 1984.

In addition to being the first woman named as a Most Wanted Terrorist, Chesimard is only the second domestic terrorist to be added to the list.

"This crime was always considered an act of domestic terrorism," said Rinaldi, who has been working the case for six years with other members of the JTTF. In the late 1960s and early 1970s, he explained, the Black Liberation Army was a "radical left wing terror group that felt justified killing law enforcement officers. Throughout the '70s," Rinaldi added, "this group conducted assaults on police stations and murdered police officers."

Chesimard's 1979 escape from prison was well planned, Rinaldi explained. "Armed domestic terrorists gained entry into the facility, neutralized the guards, broke her free, and turned her over to a nearby getaway team."

Although Chesimard has been granted asylum in Cuba, Rinaldi stressed,"This is an active investigation and will continue as such until Chesimard is apprehended."

We need your help: If you have any information concerning Joanne Chesimard, who now goes by the name Assata Shakur, please contact your local FBI office or the nearest American Embassy or Consulate.

Note: Joanne Chesimard may have been located since the above information was posted on our website. Please check our Most Wanted Terrorists webpage at www.fbi.gov/wanted/wanted_terrorists for up-to-date information.

The FBI and Leadership
Part 1: Helping Employees 'Lead Where They Stand'

FBI.gov recently sat down with Janet Kamerman, executive assistant director of our Human Resources Branch—and one of the principal architects of the FBI's Leadership Development Program—to talk about the importance of leadership at all levels of the organization.

Q: Why is leadership development so important to the FBI?

Ms. Kamerman: Leadership is important in any organization, but because of the FBI's mission to protect our national security and uphold the Constitution, effective leadership is essential. Some of the challenges we are confronted with every day as an organization are immediate and potentially deadly. We are leaders nationwide and worldwide in the law enforcement and intelligence communities. We need to continue to develop our employees to meet the challenges of today and tomorrow, as there is so much at stake.

Q: How does the FBI address leadership development in an organization of 36,000 employees?

Ms. Kamerman: The Bureau hires talented and committed individuals. Whether they are agents or professional staff, our employees usually have impressive leadership experiences prior to becoming FBI employees. We view leadership development as a continuous cycle, from your first day on the job to the day you retire. And it's not just about training. It's about being exposed to the right experiences, the right mentors—and getting honest feedback from supervisors and peers so we can self-reflect and constantly seek self improvement.

Q: The Leadership Development Program (LDP) was created in 2009. What are the program's goals?

Ms. Kamerman: The LDP was designed to put a common language around leadership and to make sure that employees—as part of the whole organization—understand the value of leadership. One of the mottos we have is "lead where you stand." Regardless of what job a person has in the Bureau, employees need to understand the importance of leadership.

Q: How would you describe the LDP?

Ms. Kamerman: The program includes courses, online tools, mentors—an entire range of resources to help

Janet Kamerman, executive assistant director of our Human Resources Branch, is a principal architect of the Bureau's Leadership Development Program.

employees explore where they are in their own leadership development, as well as where they aspire to be and how to get there. In fact, these concepts are discussed with FBI employees during their first week in the Bureau. The program provides a framework for examining and improving leadership at the individual, team, and organizational level. People usually think of training when they think of leadership development, but you can only learn so much from the classroom. We want our employees to learn from a variety of developmental experiences.

Q: Can you tell us about an employee's first week in the Bureau?

Ms. Kamerman: We call it the Onboarding New Employees (ONE) program, and it began in January 2012. Now, all new employees begin their FBI career at the FBI Academy in Quantico. People coming from Boston or Seattle—or wherever—all start together at the academy. In addition to learning the history and culture of the organization, they also get a block of training regarding leadership and the FBI's leadership doctrine. Regardless of an employee's job title—be it scientist or executive—from your very first experiences, you are taught the concept of leading where you stand. And that lays the foundation for leadership development throughout your career.

Part 2: The FBI's leadership doctrine (page 34)

The FBI and Leadership
Part 2: Character, Courage, Competence, and Collaboration

Part 2 of an interview with Janet Kamerman, executive assistant director of our Human Resources Branch, about the FBI's leadership program.

Q: The basis of the FBI's Leadership Development Program (LDP) is a leadership doctrine. How was that doctrine created?

Ms. Kamerman: The FBI's leadership doctrine, consisting of what we call the four C's—character, courage, competence, and collaboration—was developed by FBI employees through a series of workshops. The goal was to capture what our employees value in their leaders with an accountability aspect to it.

Q: Can anybody be a leader?

Ms. Kamerman: I believe leadership skills can absolutely be learned, and everybody can improve. We often say there is no finish line in leadership—it's a journey, and you have to keep learning and developing. While we hire people with previous leadership experience, we believe our programs can improve everyone's leadership skills.

Q: You have been instrumental in establishing and implementing the Bureau's leadership program. How did you become so passionate about this subject?

Ms. Kamerman: I think it probably stems from my time in the military and how leadership is embedded into the very fabric of military culture—from the very first day of service. Historically, this has not been the case in the Bureau. I recognized through my various assignments and conversations with hundreds of employees how much more effective the FBI would be if we had a comprehensive leadership development program. I was fortunate enough to be in a position to implement such a program.

Q: What do you personally look for when selecting members of your leadership team?

Ms. Kamerman: I often get asked that question. Through the years, the people that I absolutely loved working with all had three similar qualities. They were team players, they took initiative, and they made everyone else around them look better. Anyone can measure themselves against those three qualities. Leadership is not about a job title. While it is very important to get the job done, I believe what is more important is how you go about getting the job done. The reason that's important is because how we do it ensures that we can continue to do it over time. We don't just want to clear the hurdle. We want to get way over the hurdle with enough momentum so that the next hurdle—even if it's higher—will not be a problem.

Q: What are your goals for the LDP in the future?

Ms. Kamerman: The programs we have in place today—classes, seminars, mentors, onboarding programs, peer support, and other resources—and the ones we will implement going forward need to continually be reviewed and updated. Our goal is to have leadership development embedded in the FBI culture at all levels—anchored deep into our promotion processes, our human resources processes, into the very structure and fabric of the Bureau.

Police Week
Honoring the Fallen

Thousands of law enforcement officers from around the country gathered last night at the National Law Enforcement Officers Memorial for a candlelight vigil to honor fallen officers. The names of more than 19,000 men and women grace the memorial's marble walls. On Monday, 321 new names were officially added, including 120 who died last year. The names of the fallen were read aloud after thousands of participants passed a flame from candle to candle. In remarks to participants, Homeland Security Secretary Janet Napolitano saluted those who wear the badge.

"Heroes, patriots, and role models who did not flinch at the first sign of danger," she said, "but like all law enforcement, acted to protect us even though their lives were on the line."

Attorney General Eric Holder said the officers died doing what they loved.

"They helped to make this world a far better—and safer—place," Holder said. "And, despite the fact that these brave officers were taken from us far too suddenly—and far too soon—their legacies and contributions will always endure."

For more information, visit www.fbi.gov/policeweek2013.

Thousands of law enforcement officers from around the country honored their fallen colleagues during the annual Police Week in Washington, D.C.

This is the 25th year of Police Week, which began in 1962 when President John F. Kennedy signed a proclamation that designated May 15 as Peace Officers Memorial Day.

Candles and laser lights illuminate the darkness at the National Law Enforcement Officers Memorial.

A visitor makes a pencil-rubbing of a name on the memorial wall.

Internet Crime 2012
IC3 Releases Annual Report

The Internet Crime Complaint Center, or IC3, had received dozens of complaints about a St. Louis woman who was selling what she claimed were designer handbags. Buyers spent as much as $100,000 for a single bag, but ended up with either knock-off bags or sometimes nothing at all…and the woman refused to refund their money. The IC3 forwarded the complaints to the St. Louis FBI Field Office, and, after an investigation, the woman was charged with selling counterfeit goods and ultimately pled guilty last year.

This case is an example of the effectiveness of the IC3—a partnership between the FBI and the National White Collar Crime Center. Submissions to this central hub for Internet-related crime complaints can not only lead to culprits getting caught, but also help identify trends that are then posted on the IC3's website to educate the public about constantly evolving cyber threats and scams.

Today, as part of its ongoing education and prevention mission, the IC3 released its latest annual snapshot of online crime and fraud—the *2012 Internet Crime Report.* While there is no end to the variety of cyber scams, the report highlights some of the most frequent ones from 2012. Here are a few examples of what to look for to help keep you from being victimized:

- **Auto fraud:** Criminals attempt to sell vehicles that they really don't own, usually advertising them on various online platforms at prices below market value. Often the fraudsters claim they must sell the vehicles quickly because they are relocating for work, are being deployed by the military, or have a tragic family circumstance and are in need of money. And in a new twist, criminals are posing as dealers rather than individual sellers.

- **FBI impersonation e-mail scam:** The names of various government agencies and government officials have been used in spam attacks for some time, and complaints related to spam e-mail purportedly sent by the FBI continue to be reported with high frequency. These scams, which include elements of Nigerian scam letters, incorporate get-rich inheritance scenarios, bogus lottery winning notifications, and occasional extortion threats.

- **Intimidation/extortion scams:** More popular ones involve payday loan scams (harassing phone calls to victims claiming they are delinquent on loan payments), process server scams (a supposed process server shows up at a victim's house or place of employment but is willing to take a debit card number for payment in order to avoid court), and grandparent scams (fraudsters contacting elderly victims pretending to be a young family member in some sort of legal or financial crisis).

- **Scareware/ransomware:** There are different variations of these scams, but one involves victims receiving pop-up messages on their computers alerting them to purported infections that can only be fixed by purchasing particular antivirus software. Another involves malware that freezes victims' computers and displays a warning of a violation of U.S. law and directions to pay a fine to the U.S. Department of Justice.

Read more on these and other scams—as well as online crime prevention tips—in the IC3's latest report. An educated consumer is the most effective weapon against Internet fraudsters.

The Fix Was In
Crime in College Hoops

It's a cautionary tale for college and professional athletes alike.

Following a three-year FBI investigation dubbed Operation Hook Shot, eight people—including former University of San Diego (USD) basketball star Brandon Johnson, the school's all-time point and assist leader—were convicted and sentenced to federal prison terms for taking part in a sports bribery conspiracy. The eighth and final defendant, illegal bookmaker Richard Francis Garmo, was sentenced last month.

The case began—as most of our sports bribery matters do—as an organized crime investigation. In 2009, we began looking into the activities of a criminal enterprise operating in the San Diego area. Along with selling marijuana, the group was operating an illegal online gambling business. A related criminal activity, Bureau investigators discovered, was a scheme to fix USD men's basketball games.

Playing a pivotal role in the scheme was Thaddeus Brown, an assistant basketball coach at USD during the 2006-2007 season. Brown had placed bets with the illegal gambling business operated by Garmo and two partners-in-crime. Though no longer with the team, he still had contacts among the USD players. During the 2009-2010 season, he recruited Johnson—USD's starting point guard—to influence the outcome of basketball games in exchange for money. Brown was paid handsomely for his role in the conspiracy—up to $10,000 per game.

During that season, it's believed that at least four games were "fixed" with Johnson's assistance. Perhaps the senior point guard would miss a free throw now and then or draw a technical foul. Or he would just pass up a shot—at one point Johnson was heard on electronic surveillance talking about how he wouldn't shoot at the end of a particular game because it would have cost him $1,000.

The co-conspirators routinely got together to discuss the predictions of oddsmakers and to pick which games to fix. They would then make their bets—often on the other team (USD was usually favored to win)—which would enhance their winnings even more. And with Johnson manipulating the games, they usually won their bets, netting them more than $120,000.

The following season—2010-2011—Johnson had graduated, but he nonetheless tried to recruit another player to continue the scheme. His attempt ultimately failed. Brown also tried—even making attempts at two other schools—but he failed as well.

To penetrate this close-knit conspiracy, the FBI made use of its array of investigative techniques, including court-authorized wiretaps, physical surveillance, confidential informants, subpoenaed documents, and interviews. We also had the cooperation of USD officials and the NCAA. By April 2011, an indictment in conspiracy had been announced.

At the time of the indictment, U.S. Attorney Laura Duffy of the Southern District of California said, "Whether in the area of politics, law, or sports, the phrase 'the fix is in' sends chills down the spines of all Americans… Tampering with sports events strikes at the integrity of the games; this kind of betrayal is not merely disappointing—it is criminal and worthy of prosecution."

While the FBI focuses on the criminal leadership in these sorts of enterprises, athletes and coaches willing to sell out their teams for money can get caught in the net and pay the price. Our advice: Think twice before gambling with your future.

Looking for Our Children
National Missing Children's Day 2013

Earlier this month in Cleveland, three young women were freed from years of captivity after a concerned neighbor responded to an urgent call for help.

We need your help, too, in rescuing the many kids who remain far from home today. Please take a minute to look at all the faces above and on our Kidnapping and Missing Persons webpage and see if you can identify Crystal, Jaliek, Rolando, or any of the other children listed with their stories.

Also take a look at the faces of the children who have been kidnapped by a parent—Mohammad Hussain Metla, Jr. and the many other kids.

And we hope you'll visit our Violent Crimes Against Children page to learn all you can about what a dangerous world it can be for our kids…and our

Resources for Parents page to learn how to protect them in today's world.

Last: Join us in honoring the law enforcement officers and others recognized as part of National Missing Children's Day, including FBI Special Agent John D. Wydra, Jr. of our Charlotte Division. Our partners at the National Center for Missing & Exploited Children also recognized a dozen FBI employees for going "above and beyond the call of duty for safely recovering missing child or successfully resolving a child sexual exploitation case."

Note: The children pictured here may have been located since the above information was posted on our website. Please check our Wanted by the FBI website at www.fbi.gov/wanted for up-to-date information.

Wounded Warriors
Helping Injured Soldiers Continue to Serve

May 31, 2009. Eastern Afghanistan. U.S. Army Sgt. 1st Class Sean Clifton and his Special Forces team were conducting a raid against a Taliban stronghold. As an assault team leader, Clifton busted into a compound—and into a wall of enemy bullets. "I still remember everything vividly," he said, "from the time I kicked in that door to the time they Medevaced me off the battlefield."

Clifton was critically injured, with major organ damage and a shattered wrist. He eventually pulled through and spent several months at Walter Reed Medical Center in Washington, D.C. before returning to his hometown of Columbus, Ohio. There, he learned about Operation Warfighter, a Department of Defense program that places wounded service members in internship positions with federal agencies so they can contribute while healing (at the time, the program was only available in the D.C. area). Intrigued by this idea but wanting to stay in Ohio, Clifton—who had at one time considered becoming an FBI agent—called up our Cincinnati Division to see if it would be willing to do something similar. The answer? "Anything we can do to support you during your recovery."

Clifton began working as an intern in our Columbus Resident Agency, shadowing analysts and agents to help out on cases. And when his time with the military—and therefore, the internship—was up, another door opened. On April 22, 2012, Clifton became a full-time Bureau employee.

Clifton is one of many injured service members who found a place at the FBI. Various field offices—like Cincinnati—have allowed wounded warriors to intern with them over the years…and field-wide interest and support led to a national pilot program, then to the launch of the FBI's official Wounded Warrior Internship Program in August 2012.

Participants—who remain on the military's payroll—must first be approved through Operation Warfighter, have at least nine months left on their wounded warrior status, and be able to pass a full background investigation. Those selected are given assignments around the country that don't interfere with their rehabilitation and recovery and that allow them to build a résumé, explore employment

Sean Clifton was seriously injured in 2009 during a raid in Afghanistan. Today, he works for the FBI in Ohio.

interests, develop job skills, and gain federal work experience. So far, more than 50 wounded warriors have participated in the program since the pilot began in March 2011, and 15 of those interns have since come on board as full-time FBI employees.

"My goal for the program is for every field office, every Headquarters division to have at least two wounded warriors working in their space," said William McNeill, manager of our Wounded Warriors and Veterans Program and a 23-year Army veteran. "These service members still have so much more to give. They may not be able to serve in the capacity they first desired…but that sense of commitment and dedication is still there."

Four years after his injury, Clifton is grateful for all the support the FBI provided him as a wounded warrior and as a Bureau employee. "Even from day one, coming in as an intern—that helped me out not only physically, but mentally and emotionally, too, because now I have another mission and another team to be a part of. And that was just a big part of my healing."

This Memorial Day—and always—the FBI remembers those who have fallen and thanks our nation's current and former service members for all they have done and continue to do for the country.

Attempted Bombing Near Wrigley Field

Act of Terror Averted
Would-Be Bomber Sentenced in Chicago

A federal judge has sentenced an Illinois man to 23 years in prison for an attempted bombing in 2010 near Chicago's Wrigley Field that was intended to cause mass casualties and paralyze the community.

On that Saturday evening in September, while a concert was taking place at the Chicago Cubs baseball stadium, Sami Samir Hassoun placed a backpack that he thought contained a powerful bomb into a trash can on a nearby crowded street. The device was a fake—supplied by an FBI undercover agent—but had it been real, the effects would have been "horrific," according to the judge who sentenced Hassoun yesterday.

A Lebanese citizen legally living in Chicago, Hassoun never posed a danger to the public, thanks to an investigation led by our Joint Terrorism Task Force (JTTF) in Chicago. But the 25-year-old would-be terrorist had earlier told an accomplice—who was really an FBI undercover agent—that any casualties from the attack would be the inevitable result of what he termed "revolution."

Noting that the JTTF consists of Chicago police officers

and other federal, state, and local law enforcement personnel in addition to FBI agents, Special Agent Sam Hartman—who served as co-case agent with Chicago Police Detective Angel Lorenzo—explained that "a case like this doesn't have a successful outcome unless everybody pulls together. The JTTF played a key role in this investigation."

"I am proud of the work done by our investigative team in preventing Hassoun from carrying out his intended act of violence," said Cory B. Nelson, special agent in charge of our Chicago Field Office. "The FBI remains vigilant in our mission to prevent attacks against Americans."

We were initially alerted to Hassoun by an informant who warned that Hassoun was hoping to profit from committing extreme acts of violent in Chicago. "He had no qualms about potentially killing lots of people," Hartman said. "And he wanted money in return."

Hassoun pled guilty to attempted use of a weapon of mass destruction and attempted use of an explosive device, and he admitted telling a law enforcement informant that he suggested bombing the commercial area surrounding Wrigley Field. The informant later introduced Hassoun to an undercover FBI operative who posed as an accomplice. Hassoun also said he was willing to use a car bomb and to attack Chicago police officers.

On three occasions in August 2010, Hassoun videotaped potential targets around Wrigley Field, focusing on popular bars and restaurants. As he filmed, he commented on the tactical advantages and risks of an attack at the various locations.

On the night of September 18, Hassoun was ready to set his plan in motion. He took a shopping bag and a backpack from our undercover agents that he thought contained a powerful bomb. The agents said the device was surrounded by ball-bearings and that the blast could destroy half a city block. A few minutes after midnight, after he had helped set the device's timer, Hassoun placed the backpack into the trash container on the crowded sidewalk by the stadium.

"Hassoun was an example of the so-called lone offender," Hartman said. "He had no ties to organized terror groups, but he was clearly a terrorist—and potentially an extreme danger to the public. We were fortunate to have stopped him."

Preliminary 2012 Crime Statistics
Violent Crime Up, Property Crime Down

The new preliminary Uniform Crime Reporting (UCR) statistics for 2012 indicate that when compared to data for 2011, the number of violent crimes reported by law enforcement agencies around the country increased 1.2 percent during 2012, while the number of property crimes decreased 0.8 percent.

The final UCR statistics—submitted by approximately 18,000 local, state, campus, tribal, and federal law enforcement agencies from around the nation—will be released later this year in the *Crime in the United States, 2012* report.

Among the highlights of the preliminary report:

- Overall, when compared to 2011 figures, the West experienced the largest increase in reported violent crime (up 3.3 percent), and the Northeast experienced the only decrease (down 0.6 percent).

- The Northeast was the only part of the country where the four violent crime categories saw decreases across the board—murder (down 4.4 percent), forcible rapes (down 0.2 percent), robberies (down 1.4 percent), and aggravated assaults (down 0.1 percent).

- The largest rise in reported violent crime (up 3.7 percent) was in cities with populations of 500,000-999,999.

- The West experienced the only increase in reported property crime (up 5.2 percent), while the number of property crimes dropped 1.6 percent in the Northeast, 2.1 percent in the Midwest, and 3.5 percent in the South.

- The number of reported motor vehicle thefts grew by 10.6 percent in the West while showing declines in the Northeast (down 7.9 percent), the Midwest (down 3.1 percent), and the South (down 2.9 percent).

- The number of arson incidents—tallied separately from other property crimes because of various levels of participation by reporting agencies—fell 1.2 percent.

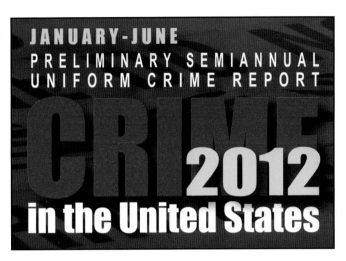

The UCR Program is a nationwide cooperative statistical effort of law enforcement agencies voluntarily reporting data on crimes brought to their attention.

The idea for the program began in the 1920s, when the International Association of Chiefs of Police—recognizing a need for national crime statistics—formed the Committee on Uniform Crime Records to develop a system. After studying state criminal codes and evaluating the recordkeeping practices in use, the committee completed a plan for crime reporting that became the foundation of the UCR Program in 1929. In January 1930, 400 cities in 43 states began participating in the program. That same year, Congress authorized the attorney general to gather crime data; the FBI was designated to serve as the national clearinghouse for the collected information.

The UCR Program's primary objective is to generate reliable statistics for use in law enforcement administration, operation, and management. Over the years, however, these statistics have become one of the country's leading social indicators and are used by criminologists, sociologists, legislators, municipal planners, the media, and other students of criminal justice for research and planning purposes.

A word of warning, though—don't draw conclusions from the data by making direct comparisons between cities or individual agencies. Valid assessments are only possible with careful study and analysis of the unique conditions that affect each law enforcement jurisdiction.

Once again, the final *Crime in the United States, 2012* report will be available later this year.

Child Abductions
When Custody Issues Lead to Violence

An analysis of recent FBI child abduction investigations has revealed a disturbing trend: Non-custodial parents are increasingly abducting and threatening to harm their own kids to retaliate against parents who were granted legal custody of the children.

"Unfortunately, the threat of violence—and death—in these cases is all too real," said Ashli-Jade Douglas, an FBI analyst in our Violent Crimes Against Children Intelligence Unit who specializes in child abduction matters. "Most non-custodial parental abductors want retaliation. They feel that if they can't have the child full time—or any amount of time—then the other parent shouldn't have the child, either."

An analysis of all FBI child abduction cases where a motivation was known shows that custodial-motivated abductions—in which a son or daughter is taken against the will of the child and the custodial parent—have increased from 9 percent in fiscal year 2010 to 50 percent in fiscal year 2012. Sometimes the motivation is to convince the custodial parent to stay in a relationship; more often it is to harm the child in an act of retaliation. This trend appears to be on the rise, Douglas said. At least 25 instances of such abductions have been reported to the FBI since October.

"Our analysis indicates that children age 3 years and younger of unwed or divorced parents are most at risk of being abducted by their non-custodial parent," Douglas added. "And the timely reporting of the abduction by the custodial parent to law enforcement is crucial in increasing the likelihood of recovering the child unharmed and apprehending the offender."

Some recent cases:

- In 2009, a non-custodial mother abducted her 8-month-old son from his custodial father in Texas. She told the father she killed the boy to prevent the father from employing his custodial rights and in retaliation for his alleged involvement with other women.

- In 2011, a 2-year-old girl was abducted by her non-custodial father in California. A week later, both were found dead. The father committed suicide after shooting his daughter.

- In 2012, a non-custodial father in Utah abducted and killed his 7- and 5-year-old sons and then committed suicide. He was angry over not being afforded sole custody of the children.

"In contrast to international parental abductions, our analysis indicates that domestic custodial abductions are more likely to have violent outcomes for children," Douglas explained, adding that a number of factors contribute to this trend. About 46 percent of American children are born to unwed parents, and 40 to 50 percent of marriages end in divorce. That usually leaves one parent with custody of the child.

Douglas offers a suggestion to help keep children safe: Custodial parents should inform schools, after-care facilities, babysitters, and others who may at times be responsible for their children about what custody agreements are in place so that kids are not mistakenly released to non-custodial parents.

"The other big takeaway from our analysis," she added, "is that law enforcement must act quickly in non-custodial abductions to keep children from being harmed. It's mind-boggling to think that a parent would hurt their child to retaliate against the other parent," Douglas said, "but in that moment, they make themselves believe that it's okay."

Civil Rights in the '60s
Part 1: Justice for Medgar Evers

The tumultuous 1960s were a pivotal time in our nation's march toward equal rights for all Americans. The following is the first in a series of stories over the next few years about landmark civil rights investigations five decades ago.

About half past midnight, a shot rang out.

It was June 12, 1963—50 years ago tomorrow—in a suburban neighborhood of Jackson, Mississippi. A 37-year-old civil rights activist named Medgar Evers had just come home after a meeting of the NAACP.

As he began the short walk up to his single-story rambler, the bullet struck Evers in the back. He staggered up to the steps of the house, then collapsed.

Across the street on a lightly wooded hill, another man jumped up in pain. The recoil from the Enfield rifle he had just fired drove the scope into his eye, badly bruising him. He dropped the weapon and fled.

Meanwhile, Evers' wife and three children—still awake after watching an important civil rights speech by President John F. Kennedy—heard the shot and quickly came outside. They were soon joined by neighbors and police. His wounds severe, Evers died within the hour.

Leading the investigation, the local police immediately found the rifle and determined that it had been recently fired. Back at the station, a fingerprint was recovered from the scope and submitted to the FBI. We connected it to a man named Byron De La Beckwith based on its similarity to his military service prints. He was arrested several days later. Beckwith, a known white supremacist and segregationist, had been asking around to find out the location of Evers' home for some time prior to the shooting.

With the obvious motive, his fingerprint on the weapon, the injury around his eye, his planning, and other factors, Beckwith clearly appeared to be the killer. In two separate trials, local prosecutors presented a strong case. A number of police, FBI experts, and others testified on different parts of the evidence against Beckwith.

But this was the 1960s, and in both trials, all-white juries did not reach a verdict. Beckwith went free.

By the early 1990s, however, the time was ripe to revisit the case. Evers' widow, Myrlie—a formidable civil rights

Medgar Evers stands near a Mississippi sign in 1958. (AP Photo)

organizer in her own right—asked local prosecutors to reopen the investigation and see if other evidence could be found. The FBI again provided its assistance. In December 1990, a new grand jury returned an indictment against Beckwith based on witnesses finally willing to tell their stories, including hearing the white supremacist brag how he had killed Medgar Evers.

This time, justice was done. Beckwith was convicted in 1994 and sentenced to life in prison.

The murder of Medgar Ever was a loss to his family, the community, and the nation. Evers was a devoted husband and father, a distinguished World War II veteran, and a pioneering civil rights leader. He served as the NAACP's first field secretary in Mississippi—organizing protests and voter registration drives, recruiting new workers into the civil rights movement, and pushing for school integration.

But his death in 1963 was not in vain. The brutal, senseless murder helped galvanize the nation in its steady march towards equality and justice. More on that later...

A Byte Out of History
The Lasting Legacy of Operation Illwind

Twenty-five years ago today, a major multi-agency investigation into defense procurement fraud—later codenamed Operation Illwind, a likely reference to an old English proverb—was announced to the world via a one-page press statement.

By the time the dust had settled several years later, the case revealed that some Defense Department employees had taken bribes from businesses in exchange for inside information on procurement bids that helped some of the nation's largest military contractors win lucrative weapons systems deals.

More than 60 contractors, consultants, and government officials were ultimately prosecuted—including a high-ranking Pentagon assistant secretary and a deputy assistant secretary of the Navy. As a monetary measure of the significance of the crimes, the case resulted in a total of $622 million worth of fines, recoveries, restitutions, and forfeitures.

The investigation began, as many cases of fraud and abuse do, when an honest individual refused to take part in criminal activity and instead contacted authorities. In 1986, a Virginia defense contractor was approached by a military consultant who said he could obtain proprietary bid information from a competitor in exchange for cash. The contractor did the right thing and reported the conversation to the FBI and the Naval Investigative Service (NIS)—now called the Naval Criminal Investigative Service, or NCIS.

The contractor agreed to cooperate and to let us monitor phone conversions he had with the consultant. After collecting enough information to determine what the consultant was up to, we confronted the man—and he agreed to cooperate as well. We soon had enough probable cause for the case's first court-authorized electronic surveillance, or wiretap, and over time developed probable cause for others.

That enabled the FBI and its partners in the case—including NIS, the Defense Criminal Intelligence Service, the Air Force Office of Special Investigations, and the Internal Revenue Service's Criminal Division—to execute more than three dozen search warrants in D.C. and 12 states on June 14, 1988. These searches of the offices of defense contractors, consultants, and government officials yielded a mountain of evidence, including financial documents.

A slew of indictments followed, and many of the defendants—faced with overwhelming evidence, including recorded telephone conversations where they had discussed their crimes—simply pled guilty.

The legacy of Operation Illwind is significant. The scandal so shocked the nation that just five months after the case became public, new rules governing federal procurement were put into place. The Procurement Integrity Act, amended in 1996, remains the law of the land.

The multi-agency investigation was also ground-breaking for the Bureau, especially in its use of court-authorized electronic surveillance—one of the first times we had used this tool so extensively in a white-collar crime investigation. A quarter century later, the case remains the largest and most successful investigation of defense procurement fraud in U.S. history.

Building on lessons learned from the case, the FBI continues to work with its partners to investigate defense procurement fraud and other government scams through our public corruption program, which addresses the FBI's number one criminal priority. Using sophisticated and traditional investigative techniques, we remain committed to exposing procurement fraud not only in the Washington, D.C. area, but also around the nation.

Top Ten at 500
Two New Fugitives Added to List

The FBI's Ten Most Wanted Fugitives program—an iconic symbol of the Bureau's crime-fighting ability recognized around the world—has reached a milestone with the naming of the 500th fugitive to the Top Ten list.

Jose Manuel Garcia Guevara and Walter Lee Williams—numbers 499 and 500, respectively—are the latest fugitives to be named to the list that was established more than six decades ago and has included notorious criminals such as bank robber Willie Sutton, serial killer Ted Bundy, Centennial Park bomber Eric Ruldoph, and terrorist Osama bin Laden.

During a ceremony held today near FBI Headquarters at the Newseum—a museum dedicated to news and journalism—FBI Assistant Director of Public Affairs Mike Kortan noted, "The Top Ten program relies heavily on the help of citizens and the media. Without their help over the years, the FBI could not have located many of these individuals."

Between the two of them, the fugitives named today are wanted for a combination of crimes including rape, murder, and the sexual exploitation of children. Rewards are being offered for information leading to the apprehension of both men.

"These individuals are a dangerous menace to society," said Ron Hosko, assistant director of our Criminal Investigative Division. "That's what got criminals on the Top Ten list 63 years ago, and that's why we put them on the list today."

Jose Manuel Garcia Guevara is wanted for unlawful flight to avoid prosecution. In 2008, he allegedly broke into the mobile home of a 26-year-old woman in Lake Charles, Louisiana and raped and stabbed her to death in front of her 4-year-old stepson. Guevara is believed to have fled to Dallas, Texas and then potentially on to Mexico.

Walter Lee Williams, a former university professor, is wanted for allegedly sexually exploiting children and traveling abroad for the purpose of engaging in illicit sexual acts with children. Williams has an extensive history of travel throughout Southeast Asia—specifically the Philippines. He may also travel to Mexico and Peru. Both Williams and Guevara are considered to be extremely dangerous.

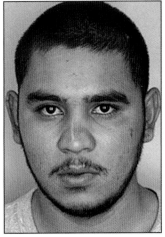 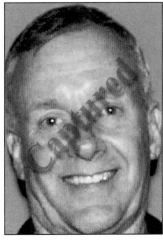

Jose Manuel Garcia Guevara   Walter Lee Williams

Since its creation in 1950, the intent of the Top Ten list has been to seek the help of the public and the media to catch some of the nation's worst offenders. That strategy has paid off. Of the 500 fugitives who have been named to the list, 469 have been apprehended or located. Of those, 155 fugitives have been captured or located as a direct result of citizen cooperation.

"This has been a tremendously successful program," Hosko said, "but one that is dependent on the willingness of concerned citizens with information to come forward and offer us their assistance."

We need your help. If you have any information about Guevara or Williams, please contact your local FBI office, the nearest U.S. Embassy or Consulate, or submit a tip on our website.

06/19/13 Update: Walter Lee Williams has been captured.

Note: Jose Manuel Garcia Guevara may have been located since the above information was posted on our website. Please check our Ten Most Wanted Fugitives webpage at www.fbi.gov/wanted/topten for up-to-date information.

James Comey speaks at the White House following his nomination by President Barack Obama to be the next Director of the FBI when Director Robert S. Mueller's term ends on September 4.

New FBI Director
President Nominates James B. Comey at White House Ceremony

President Barack Obama today nominated James B. Comey to serve as the next Director of the FBI. Comey must be confirmed by the U.S. Senate before taking office.

"Jim is exceptionally qualified to handle the full range of challenges faced by today's FBI," the president said during a ceremony held at the White House. "I am confident that Jim will be a leader who understands how to keep America safe and to stay true to our founding ideals no matter what the future may bring."

"I want to commend the president for the choice of Jim Comey as the next Director of the FBI," said current Director Robert S. Mueller. "I have had the opportunity to work with Jim for a number of years at the Department of Justice, and I have found him to be a man of honesty, dedication, and integrity. His experience, his judgment, and his strong sense of duty will benefit not only the Bureau but the country as a whole."

Comey served as deputy attorney general under the George W. Bush administration from December 2003 until August 2005, running the day-to-day operations of the Department of Justice. Prior to that, he was U.S. Attorney for the Southern District of New York, where he prosecuted a number of major terrorism and criminal cases. From 1996 to 2001, Comey worked in the U.S. Attorney's Office for the Eastern District of Virginia. He has extensive industry experience as well, serving as general counsel and senior vice president for Lockheed Martin and general counsel for the investment firm Bridgewater Associates.

"Just as important as Jim's extraordinary experience is his character," President Obama said. "Jim understands that in times of crisis, we aren't judged solely by how many plots we disrupt or how many criminals we bring to justice—we are also judged by our commitment to the Constitution that we've sworn to defend and to the values and civil liberties that we've pledged to protect."

Mueller steps down September 4 after serving 12 years—his original 10-year term plus a two-year extension proposed by the White House and approved by Congress in 2011. "I want to take this opportunity to thank the men and women of the FBI," Mueller said. "Through their hard work, their dedication, and their adaptability, the FBI is better able to predict and prevent terrorism and crime."

If his nomination is confirmed, Comey will be the 11th Director in the FBI's 105-year history—the 7th since the J. Edgar Hoover era. When it began in 1908, the Bureau's leader was called "Chief." Since 1919, the organization's top administrator has been called "Director." The Director has answered directly to the attorney general since the 1920s and by law is appointed by the president and confirmed by the Senate. In 1976, in reaction to the extraordinary 48-year term of Hoover, Congress passed a law limiting the FBI Director to a single term of no longer than 10 years.

Race Against Time
Holiday Bomb Threat Averted

It was one of those cases like you might see on TV or in the movies—where the FBI and its partners work feverishly behind the scenes, racing to stop bombs from going off and lives from possibly being lost.

But this was real—and the stakes were high. The target was one of the nation's largest retailers in one of America's most populated areas. And the day of reckoning was Black Friday, the busiest shopping day of the year.

It all started last October 15, when the Home Depot in Huntington, New York—a town on the north shore of Long Island—received an ominous anonymous note. The sender demanded $2 million or he would "shut down" three Home Depot stores on Long Island the day after Thanksgiving by remotely setting off bombs filled with roofing nails using a cell phone. As proof of his ability to hide a bomb, he said that he had planted a live device in the Huntington store's lighting department.

The man wasn't bluffing. Home Depot immediately contacted the Suffolk County Police Department, which found an operational pipe bomb hidden within a light fixture inside a box on a shelf. Bomb techs rendered it harmless through a controlled detonation.

Suffolk County and FBI bomb techs later agreed that if a store employee or customer had come across the bomb and picked it up, it could have exploded. And the device made it clear that the bomb-maker knew what he was doing.

Two days later, the man called Home Depot and repeated his demands. Five days later, the store received a second letter, this time lowering the ransom to $1 million and setting up a "money drop" for October 26.

According to the criminal complaint filed in the case, on the day of the money drop, the bomber intended to be "wired up like a Christmas tree" with "2 devices strapped to a belt and 1 to a neck chain I will be wearing, wired together and attached to a deadman switch in my hand." The man also stated that "to keep from being shot at a distance," he intended to place an additional explosive device in a Home Depot store.

But just before the scheduled money drop, the would-be bomber made a second phone call to Home Depot to call it off…for the time being.

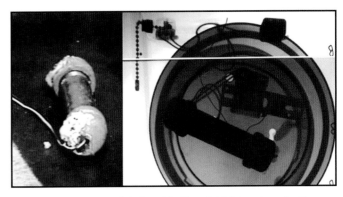

The explosive device, left, found inside a light fixture box at a Home Depot store in Long Island, New York. An X-ray shows the device inside the actual light fixture.

All the while, a multi-agency team of investigators from federal, state, and local law enforcement were compiling a list of suspects and working to narrow it down. A prime suspect soon emerged—Daniel Patrick Sheehan, an employee of the Home Depot store in nearby Deer Park.

On November 7—after using a variety of innovative investigative techniques—law enforcement located and arrested Sheehan in the vicinity of one of the Long Island Home Depot locations. Found in Sheehan's possession was the cell phone used to make the threatening phone calls to the store.

On June 17, 2013, Sheehan was convicted by a federal jury of extorting his employer and using a destructive device. As then-FBI New York Acting Assistant Director in Charge Mary Galligan said after Sheehan's arrest, "Whatever his motivation …[Sheehan's] scheme caused economic loss, was a huge drain on law enforcement resources, and threatened the safety of untold numbers of innocent people, any one of which is unacceptable."

FBI agents at the Oklahoma horse farm that served as a money laundering front for Los Zetas.

Equine Crime
A Horse Farm of a Different Color

By outward appearances, the owner of an Oklahoma farm bought American quarter horses to train, breed, and race. But Jose Trevino Morales, the brother of two leaders of the violent and powerful Mexican drug cartel Los Zetas, was not just in the horse business: He was using the farm as a front to launder millions of dollars of the cartel's illicit profits.

A three-year investigation led by the FBI resulted in convictions recently in federal court against Trevino and three others for conspiracy to commit money laundering. The case was significant because it revealed the reach and influence of Los Zetas in the U.S.—and it also illustrated how effective our investigators have become at targeting the cartel's leaders.

"Core family members of the cartel and key business partners were impacted by this case," said Special Agent David Villarreal, who supervised the investigation from our Laredo Resident Agency in Texas. "The FBI is targeting the highest echelons of the cartel's leadership, and that sends a strong message not only to the cartel but to the people who are laundering their money on the American side of the border."

The investigation, conducted through the Department of Justice-run Organized Crime Drug Enforcement Task Force (OCDETF) program, showed that since 2008, Trevino and his associates bought and sold racehorses with Los Zetas drug money using shell companies and front men. Testimony at trial revealed that during a 30-month period, the defendants spent $16 million in New Mexico, Oklahoma, California, and Texas on the horse farm operation.

U.S. Attorney Robert Pitman, who prosecuted the case, said after the trial, "The government was able to show how the corrupting influence of drug cartels has extended into the United States with cartel bosses using an otherwise legitimate domestic industry to launder proceeds from drug trafficking and other crimes."

Investigators traced "upwards of $22 million that was laundered and shipped back to Mexico," Villarreal said. "And that was just a piece of the operation that we used as a snapshot to prove our case in court."

Villarreal believes that dismantling the horse farm operation will hamper the cartel's ability to launder money, and that, in turn, will help restrict its U.S. operations. As part of the case, the government seized 455 horses and will seek a judgment in an upcoming civil trial that will include forfeitures of cash, U.S. real estate, and three jets that could total more than $70 million.

In Laredo, on the South Texas border, "the Zetas are the main criminal threat, responsible for most of the violence, kidnappings, human and drug smuggling, and related crime," Villarreal explained. "Across the border in Mexico, they have bombed police stations and assassinated numerous public officials." This cartel, he said, "has committed countless atrocities, and they are responsible for destabilizing the border."

He added that everyone on the task force—including the Internal Revenue Service, the U.S. Attorney's Office for the Western District of Texas, the Drug Enforcement Administration, and other federal, state, and local law enforcement agency partners—worked hard to make the case against Trevino and his associates.

"Personally," said Villarreal, who grew up in the region, "it is very rewarding to be able to bring justice to these ruthless people and to help stop their U.S. operations."

Bomb Technicians
An Equitable Partnership Between FBI and Navy

Special Agent James Verdi has traveled to Afghanistan, Iraq, and the Horn of Africa to study battlefield explosives. The FBI bomb technician embedded with the military and applied his specialized skills there to find signatures and forensic material on bomb fragments and unexploded devices that helped the military piece together a clearer picture of its adversaries.

As a certified bomb technician in the Bureau's San Diego Field Office, Verdi is a long way from the battlefield today. But he still rolls out regularly with a Navy explosive ordnance disposal (EOD) unit—this one based on Coronado Island just outside San Diego. During training missions, Navy ships and planes drop live ammo on San Clemente Island 70 miles off the coast. Clearing the remnants is the job of the EOD technicians. Verdi often joins them so he can see firsthand how current military technicians operate in the field and what they are likely to encounter on the ground.

"They invite us along on a lot of their training exercises to do range clearance operations," said Verdi. "That teaches us the military ordnance side of the house: what bombs, artillery rounds, and munitions look like so we can deal with them better if we see them."

The working relationship in San Diego started about a decade ago, when the wars in Iraq and Afghanistan were ramping up and the military and FBI saw mutual benefits to sharing their unique skills and knowledge. For the FBI, which has played a growing investigative role in the war theaters by analyzing improvised explosive devices (IEDs) to help pinpoint their sources, the relationship is key because the military most frequently encounters IEDs. For EOD technicians, training with the FBI has opened a window on how explosives can be exploited for evidence, like at a crime scene.

"Our jobs are very similar, although we have more experience with military ordnance and they have much more expertise in the counterterrorism portions of the job—like explosives chemical analysis, explosives precursor knowledge, and so forth," said Lt. Abe Kim of the Navy's EOD detachment on Coronado Island. "We each bring different things to the table."

Training together is a rule in the tight community of 468 bomb squads and more than 3,200 non-military

bomb technicians across the country. To ensure consistency, every bomb technician is certified—and recertified every three years—through the Hazardous Devices School at Redstone Arsenal in Alabama, run by the FBI and the Army. Training with EOD techs, says Special Agent Steve Diaczyszyn—who supervises all of the Bureau's special agent bomb technicians—is a key facet of the job.

"You never know when the public safety bomb techs and the EOD technicians are going to have to work together in the interest of public safety," Diaczyszyn said. He added that every field office bomb technician knows their EOD counterpart because the military takes the lead when a case involves ordnance without a terrorism nexus.

Verdi and his team respond to more than 200 calls a year for incidents or suspicious packages. Every experience is unique, he says, so it's important to share what you learn. Your life—and the lives of your partners—depends on it.

"That's one of the most important things we get out of working and training together with the Navy," said Verdi. "You have to earn their trust. And they have to know exactly how you're going to perform downrange in stressful environments, especially when you're in the combat theater. We train regularly so they know exactly how we are going to react. And they can depend on us when they need to."

Terror Financing
Tracking the Money Trails

The U.S.-born radical cleric Anwar al-Awlaki once wrote an essay called "44 Ways to Support Jihad." Five of his top 10 strategies focused on the same topic—money.

It's not surprising. Money fuels the operations of terrorists. It's needed to communicate, buy supplies, fund planning, and carry out acts of destruction.

But there's a flip side to this proverbial coin. In the shadowy, secretive world of terrorists, this spending leaves a trail—a trail that we can follow to help expose extremists and their network of supporters…sometimes before they can strike.

That's why shortly after 9/11, we established the Terrorist Financing Operations Section (TFOS). Within the FBI, TFOS is responsible for following the money, providing financial expertise on our terrorism investigations, and centralizing efforts to identity extremists and shut down terrorism financing in specific cases. More recently, TFOS has adopted a broader strategy to identity, disrupt, and dismantle **all** terrorist-related financial and fundraising activities. A key element is using financial intelligence to help identify previously unknown terrorist cells, recognize potential terrorist activity/planning, and develop a comprehensive threat picture.

It's challenging work. The dollar amounts can be small—for example, the Oklahoma City bombing cost a little over $4,000 to carry out, the attack on the USS Cole about $10,000, and the London subway bombings around $14,000. At the same time, terror groups can obtain funding from seemingly legitimate sources— like donations, community solicitations, and other fundraising activities. They can also generate money from criminal activities such as kidnappings, extortion, smuggling, and fraud. And their financial networks—their methods and means of moving money—use both formal systems (i.e., banks, licensed money remitters, and the Internet) and informal systems (i.e., unlicensed money remitters and money couriers).

But TFOS and investigators from our 103 Joint Terrorism Task Forces around the country are able to apply certain financial investigative techniques—like credit history checks, reviews of banking activity, and government database inquiries—to counterterrorism cases to help track terror money trails. These techniques generate a treasure trove of intelligence: personal information like citizenship, date of birth, and phone numbers; non-terrorism-related criminal activity; previously known business and personal associations; travel patterns; communication patterns; and suspicious purchases.

These techniques can also help link previously unrelated cases, create historical timelines, and generate additional leads that allow investigators to use more sophisticated techniques like court-authorized electronic surveillance.

In addition to working with FBI field offices, the men and women of TFOS—experienced agents, intelligence analysts, forensic accountants, and other professionals—handle critical outreach duties. They coordinate efforts with the U.S. intelligence community and—through FBI legal attachés—our global intelligence and law enforcement partners. They work jointly with domestic law enforcement and regulatory communities. And, in conjunction with the Treasury Department's Financial Crimes Enforcement Network (FINCEN), they conduct liaison with the financial services sector.

TFOS chief Jane Rhodes-Wolfe believes that the combined efforts of the financial industry, international partners, and federal, state, and local agencies "have established an increasingly difficult environment for terrorist financiers to operate in undetected…and ensure an ongoing and coordinated approach to terrorist financing to help prevent future terrorist attacks against the U.S."

Latent Hit of the Year Award
Fingerprint Tool Helps Solve 1999 Murder

In September 2001, a California sheriff's department linked up electronically with the FBI's Integrated Automated Fingerprint Identification System, or IAFIS, through the California Department of Justice. To test the system, the department selected as its inaugural submission a latent print found at the crime scene of an unsolved 1999 murder. IAFIS returned several possible matches, and subsequent investigation led to the arrest and guilty plea of the man responsible.

And three key individuals involved in this case were recently selected for the 2013 Latent "Hit of the Year" Award, given annually by our Criminal Justice Information Services Division to latent print examiners and law enforcement officers for their efforts to solve major crimes using IAFIS latent print services.

How the investigation began. On December 2, 1999, the San Bernardino Police Department responded to a call regarding an unresponsive male on the floor of a jewelry store. The victim was identified as 74-year-old Marshall Adams, a well known jeweler who worked for 25 years as a teacher before opening his own store.

San Bernardino Police detective John Munoz headed the investigation, with assistance from the Scientific Investigations Division of the San Bernardino County Sheriff's Department. Identification technicians—including Randy Beasley—collected latent fingerprints, palmprints, and blood evidence obtained from a knife, doors, and a store catalog. Beasley also discovered a bloody palmprint on the victim's face. Adams had been brutally beaten and stabbed, and his wallet and several pieces of display case jewelry were missing.

The sheriff's department processed the crime scene evidence and searched all latent prints against their own databases. One possible suspect was identified but then cleared. With no other leads, the case went cold.

IAFIS proves its mettle. Then, in September 2001, the San Bernardino County Sheriff's Department joined the IAFIS network and sent in a fingerprint from the Adams case—specifically, a latent print taken from a jewelry catalog. Shortly thereafter, IAFIS responded with a list of possible candidates. Supervising fingerprint examiner

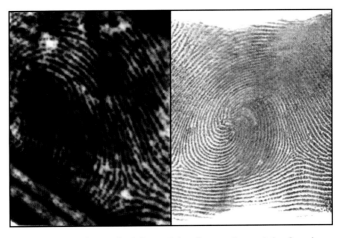

The latent print on the left was taken from a store catalog found at the scene of a 1999 murder of a jeweler. On the right is the fingerprint from IAFIS matched to the latent print by a San Bernardino County Sheriff's Department fingerprint examiner.

James Nursall concluded that the latent print evidence was a match to one of the candidates—Jad Salem—who, according to IAFIS, had been arrested in Texas two weeks after Adams' murder. He had been stopped for a traffic violation but was then arrested on a drug charge, and Texas authorities entered Salem's prints into IAFIS.

Detective Munoz located Salem in San Bernardino. After being advised of the fingerprint evidence against him, Salem agreed to provide his fingerprints and palmprints for comparison against latent evidence collected from the crime scene. Fingerprint examiner Nursall concluded that Salem's prints matched the latent prints found on the jewelry store door and on the victim's face.

Salem was arrested and charged with Adams' murder. During an interview, Salem admitted being at the crime scene but claimed to have only been a witness. He could not, however, explain how his palmprint left a bloody impression on the victim's face. And according to courtroom proceedings, Salem and Adams had met several times to discuss the purchase of an engagement ring.

In the face of this overwhelming evidence, Salem pled guilty and was sentenced to 32 years in prison. Proof positive of the key role that technology can play in identifying dangerous criminals and bringing them to justice.

Left: Map of Pennsylvania and New Jersey by H.S. Tanner

Map Quest
Seeking Owners of Stolen Artwork

After a well-known dealer of rare maps was caught stealing from a Yale University library in 2006, a subsequent FBI investigation revealed that the man had stolen antique maps and other valuable items from institutions around the world. Most of the pilfered material was eventually returned to its rightful owners—but not all of it.

We are still in possession of 28 rare maps and books—some dating to the 17th century—and we would like to return them. To that end, we are posting pictures and information about the items in the accompanying photo gallery in the hopes that the individuals or institutions who own them will come forward to claim them.

"These items have been legally forfeited to the U.S. government," said Bonnie Magness-Gardiner, who manages the FBI's Art Theft Program. "Technically, they belong to the Bureau now, but we don't want to keep them. Even though we have tried to find the rightful owners over the years, we are making another attempt."

After Edward Forbes Smiley, III was arrested for the Yale library theft, he admitted stealing and selling nearly 100 rare maps from international collections over a period of seven years. With Smiley's cooperation, we tracked down most of the dealers and collectors who purchased the approximately $3 million worth of stolen material. But returning the maps to their homes proved to be a daunting task.

In many cases, the maps were cut from books with a razor and trimmed so they didn't look like they came from

books. Some of the maps had different titles—many in Latin—and could have come from several known copies of the same book. To further complicate matters, many libraries weren't even aware they were missing items until we contacted them.

"These maps aren't vehicles with identification numbers stamped on them," Special Agent Stephen J. Kelleher, who led the 2006 investigation, said at the time. Special Agent Lisa MacNamara, who is working the case now from our New Haven Division, added, "Our hope is that by reaching out to the public in this way, we can get these historical items back to where they belong."

The items still in our possession include rare maps such as an 18th century depiction of the United States and a 1683 street plan of Philadelphia, as well as several antique books.

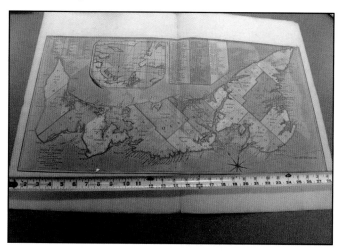

Jeffrey's Atlas, "St John Newfoundland"

If you believe that one of the maps or books shown in the gallery was stolen from your collection, please contact Special Agent MacNamara at (203) 503-5268 or send an e-mail to artwork@ic.fbi.gov. To claim any of the items, you will need to provide evidence of ownership and positively identify the item in question. That might include—but is not limited to—giving a description of special markings or stamps, wear patterns, specific damage, or other detailed information.

Note: To view the gallery, visit www.fbi.gov/recoveredart.

Homegrown Terrorism
Self-Radicalized American Incited Violent Jihad Online

Those who have met Emerson Begolly in person might describe him as a shy young man. But online, the 24-year-old was the complete opposite—he forcefully incited jihadist violence against Americans and Jews. And when FBI agents attempted to talk to him in 2011, he reached for a loaded handgun in his pocket and then bit the agents who disarmed him.

Today, a federal judge sentenced Begolly to eight years and six months in prison for soliciting others to engage in acts of terrorism within the United States and for using a firearm in relation to an assault on FBI agents. Begolly pled guilty in August 2011 after being indicted less than a month earlier.

"This is a guy who definitely had the potential to hurt people," said Special Agent Blake McGuire, who led part of the investigation from our Pittsburgh office. "He was a disaffected U.S. citizen who was susceptible to the message of violent extremism, and he became self-radicalized on the Internet. That type of offender—the so-called lone wolf—is extremely dangerous," McGuire added, "because they can be difficult to discover before they resort to violence."

Begolly came to the FBI's attention in 2010 when he began posting violent material on an Islamic extremist Internet forum. Using the pseudonym Abu Nancy, the Pennsylvania resident and occasional college student solicited fellow jihadists to use firearms and explosives against American police stations, post offices, Jewish schools and daycare centers, military facilities, train lines, and water plants. He further urged his audience to "write their legacy in blood" and promised a special place in the afterlife for violent action in the name of Allah.

Members of the Bureau's Joint Terrorism Task Forces in Pittsburgh and in Northern Virginia worked on the case with U.S. attorneys in both jurisdictions. "We all shared the same concern," McGuire said, "that something might trigger this young man to carry out his own personal jihad."

Begolly was under surveillance during the summer of 2010 when he legally purchased an assault weapon. Several months later, he escalated his online postings by soliciting jihadists to violence by posting a manual on how to manufacture a bomb.

Shortly after the bomb-making post, agents obtained search warrants for the homes of Begolly's parents, where he often stayed. While the searches were being conducted, two other agents approached Begolly at a fast food restaurant near Pittsburgh to speak with him. That's when he reached for the loaded handgun in his pocket. As the agents subdued him, he bit their fingers, trying to free himself and reach for his gun. His actions were consistent with a previous online post in which he urged jihadists not to be taken alive by law enforcement and to always carry a loaded firearm.

"When you combine troubling rhetoric that escalates with weapons, it poses a tremendous threat to public safety," McGuire said. "Fortunately, we headed off any potential danger before it happened."

Cheating in Contracts
A $30 Million Case of Corruption

It's been billed as the "largest domestic bribery and bid-rigging scheme in the history of federal contracting cases."

Specifically, over a five-year period, more than $30 million was illegally siphoned from federal coffers by a ring of crooked public officials and government contractors in the D.C. area operating via bribes, kickbacks, and other dirty dealings.

A big fix, especially in lean budget times. The plot was thickening, too—a billion-dollar government contract was about to be steered illegally into favored hands in exchange for sizeable payments under the table.

But ultimately the hammer fell, and fell hard, following a massive, multi-year investigation by the FBI and its partners called Five Aces (a reference to cheating by stacking the deck) that came to light in October 2011 after the first arrests. A total of 15 federal employees and contractors—plus one company, Nova Datacom—have since pled guilty. That includes the mastermind of the conspiracy, Kerry Khan, who just last week was sentenced to nearly 20 years in prison.

Khan, while serving as a program manager and contracting officer's technical representative for the U.S. Army Corps of Engineers, cooked up the bribery scheme in 2006 with his co-worker Michael Alexander to take their own piece of the contracting pie.

The case evolved into a complicated conspiracy, involving six different companies and several shady practices. The FBI began its investigation in the summer of 2009, when we received a tip indicating that an area business was submitting phony references and evaluations to boost its chances of getting government contracts. The company, we discovered, also had a disabled veteran falsely posing as its owner—which gave it an advantage under federal contracting laws.

We soon learned that Khan and his criminal colleague had created a network of crooked contractors who agreed to pay them bribes and kickbacks in exchange for winning deals. In most of those cases, the contracts were fulfilled and the work done, but often times there were extra charges disguised as "overhead" on the bills… and most of that money ended up in Khan's pockets. In other instances, Khan awarded contracts to straw subcontractors and paid fake invoices submitted by the fictitious companies.

For the members of the criminal conspiracy, it was a lucrative enterprise—especially for Khan, who was paid, directly and indirectly, more than $12 million. Khan used the money to live large: in addition to paying off his mortgage and remodeling his house, he purchased flat screen TVs, computers, luxury watches, airline tickets, accommodations in five-star hotels, high-end liquor, and a dozen properties in three states. And apparently, money is thicker than blood in some cases— Khan got his son and brother involved in the scheme (both have since pled guilty).

Five Aces was a multi-agency undertaking from the start, with the FBI and its partners uncovering vital evidence using sophisticated investigative techniques, including consensual recordings by cooperating witnesses and court-authorized wiretaps. We heard details about crimes directly from the mouths of the criminals committing them.

Justice has been served, and, just as importantly, more than $32 million is being rightfully returned to the U.S. government and the American people. It's another case in point as to why the FBI continues to focus squarely on public corruption as its top criminal investigative priority.

All in the Family
Part 1: Husband, Wife, and Son Stole Millions from Armored Cars

A shaken driver handcuffed to the door of his armored car. Millions of dollars stolen. An investigation involving turncoat family members, and an indictment handed down just days before the statute of limitations ran out.

It may sound like the plot of a Hollywood thriller, but that's how the long saga of the Cabello family unfolded—in a crime spree spanning more than a decade that finally landed Archie and Marian Cabello and their son, Vincent, behind bars.

It all began in 1995 in Milwaukee, Wisconsin, while Archie was employed as an armored car driver. One day, he arranged for his wife to meet him on his route, where he handed her a bag containing more than $157,000. He later told the police that the money had simply disappeared.

Three years later, the couple recruited their son into the family crime business. Vincent took a job working as a vault clerk for an armored truck company. One night, Archie—wearing a hat and fake beard and using a BB gun as a prop—staged a robbery at the company during his son's work shift, cuffing Vincent's hands and legs. While Vincent played the victim, Archie made off with $730,000 in cash. Authorities never charged anyone in the 1995 or 1998 thefts.

The Cabellos moved to Portland, Oregon in 1999, and father and son took jobs working for security or delivery companies. The family seemed to lay low until 2005, when Archie took a new job as an armored truck driver. By December of that year—believing they had gotten away with the two previous robberies—the family was ready for another heist.

On December 6, 2005, Archie was driving an armored car loaded with $7 million in cash, including two shrink-wrapped bricks containing $1.5 million each. Using disposable cell phones provided by Marian, father and son arranged a meeting point, where Archie passed off both bundles of cash—$3 million in hundred-dollar bills—to Vincent, who concealed it in a duffel bag. Playing the victim this time, Archie drove the armored truck several blocks away, handcuffed himself to the truck door, and flagged down a passerby to call police. Vincent, meanwhile, made his getaway and stashed the loot in a safe deposit box in Bellevue, Washington.

Local authorities and FBI investigators called in to help with the case immediately became suspicious when they learned that Archie and Vincent had been "victims" of similar crimes in Milwaukee six years earlier. A search warrant executed about a week after the Portland heist turned up credit cards and cash, but not enough to connect the family to the robbery.

"We knew the Cabellos weren't being honest about what happened," said Special Agent Kenneth O'Connor, who worked the case from our Portland Division, "but initially, there was not a lot of evidence linking them to the crime." After months of surveillance and investigation, the case grew cold.

But thanks to the diligence of our investigators, along with the Internal Revenue Service and the U.S. Attorney's Office in Portland, the Cabellos' luck was about to run out…

Part 2: Following the money (page 56)

All in the Family
Part 2: On the Trail of Armored Car Robbers

Beginning in 1995, the Cabello family—husband Archie, wife Marian, and son Vincent—had managed to steal nearly $4 million in cash from armored car companies in three robberies over a period of 10 years, all while eluding authorities. But their crimes were about to earn them something they hadn't bargained for—justice.

Our agents had suspected the family since a 2005 Portland, Oregon armored car robbery in which $3 million in cash was stolen, but there was not enough evidence to charge the Cabellos with the crime—that is, until we started to follow their spending habits.

"They were spending money they didn't have," said Special Agent Kenneth O'Connor, who joined the case in 2008 from our Portland Division. "They bought things and paid rent and utilities with more than 50 credit cards, and then used money orders purchased with the stolen cash to pay off the credit cards."

O'Connor knew the case would require a lot of sophisticated financial investigation, so he asked the Internal Revenue Service for assistance. "I knew the IRS was well-versed in that kind of work," O'Connor said, "and from the beginning, it was a great partnership."

The joint investigation revealed that the Cabellos had spent more than $245,000 between 2006 and 2009 but claimed less than $35,000 in income on tax returns. The family had hoped to avoid suspicion by sticking to mostly small-scale purchases like cigars, running shoes, and used vehicles—but the numbers didn't lie.

A few days before the statute of limitations ran out in December 2010, a federal grand jury handed down a 51-count indictment accusing Archie, Vincent, and Marian of conspiring to stage the Portland robbery and the two Milwaukee thefts and to launder the proceeds. Though released pending trial, the three were ordered to surrender their passports and wear electronic monitoring devices.

"The U.S. Attorney's Office in Portland did an outstanding job of devising a prosecution strategy and presenting evidence to the grand jury about all the robberies," O'Connor explained, "so that everyone understood how brazen and far-reaching these crimes were."

In February 2012, Vincent—who had started to turn his life around while on pre-trial release, taking college classes and getting engaged to be married—began cooperating and led investigators to nearly $2 million in cash in a safe deposit box.

"That was a critical point in the case," O'Connor said. "The safe deposit box was set up under an assumed name—there was nothing that connected it to the family, and we hadn't discovered it."

Faced with more than 30,000 pages of evidence against him plus the testimony of his co-conspirators (Marian had also eventually agreed to testify against her husband), Archie pled guilty to each of the eight substantive counts the morning his trial was set to begin. In March 2013, a judge sentenced him to 20 years in federal prison for his role in the decade-long crime spree. Marian and Vincent each received 15-month sentences. The family was ordered to pay restitution of nearly $4 million to the victims of the thefts.

"Most Americans get by with hard work and sacrifice," said FBI Portland Special Agent in Charge Greg Fowler at the time of the sentencing. "The Cabellos spent years scamming the system, stealing millions of dollars to pay their bills. Now they are rightly being held accountable for their crimes thanks to the great partnership between the FBI and the IRS."

Operation Cross Country
Recovering Victims of Child Sex Trafficking

Operation Cross Country—a three-day nationwide enforcement action focusing on underage victims of prostitution—has concluded with the recovery of 105 sexually exploited children and the arrests of 150 pimps and other individuals.

The sweep took place in 76 cities and was carried out by the FBI in partnership with local, state, and federal law enforcement agencies and the National Center for Missing & Exploited Children (NCMEC) as part of the Bureau's Innocence Lost National Initiative. It is the seventh and largest such enforcement action to date.

"Child prostitution remains a persistent threat to children across America," said Ron Hosko, assistant director of the FBI's Criminal Investigative Division. "This operation serves as a reminder that these abhorrent crimes can happen anywhere and that the FBI remains committed to stopping this cycle of victimization and holding the criminals who profit from this exploitation accountable."

Since its creation in 2003, the Innocence Lost National Initiative has resulted in the identification and recovery of more than 2,700 children who have been sexually exploited. Behind those numbers are the stories of real victims.

Alex was one such victim. At age 15, faced with a difficult family situation at home, she decided to leave and stay with a girlfriend and then an aunt. When that didn't work out, she found herself on the street—with an abusive boyfriend who wanted to pimp her out.

"You learn quickly that the only people who are really willing to feed you, clothe you, and shelter you are your parents," she said. "So I had to figure something out."

Alex was 16 years old and desperate. She turned to prostitution and later fell under the influence of a pimp and her family. "At first it was terrifying, and then you just kind of become numb to it," she said. "You put on a whole different attitude—like a different person. It wasn't me. I know that. Nothing about it was me."

Two years later, Alex bravely contacted the FBI, and her cooperation helped us send two pimps to prison and facilitate the recovery of other underage victims. Today, with support from the Bureau's Office for Victim

Assistance, Alex is turning her life around. She earned her high school diploma, is living on her own, and has plans to attend college. She wants to become an advocate for young victims of sexual exploitation.

"What happened to me happened, and I can't change it," she said. "I can only change my future."

Special Agent Kurt Ormberg, who helped recover Alex and put her pimp behind bars, explained that children who are most susceptible to sexual exploitation have a void in their lives. "That void might be related to family, food, or shelter, but it's a void that needs to be filled, and pimps fill it." And after they nurture their victims, he said, they sexually exploit them. "Too often," Ormberg added, "these young victims don't think they have anywhere else to turn."

"I was very lucky to be able to walk away," Alex said. "I never got hurt, so I'm really, really lucky. I'm one of the few that can say that." Without the help of the FBI, she added, "I probably would have ended up dead."

Forty-seven FBI divisions took part in Operation Cross Country VII, along with more than 3,900 local, state, and federal law enforcement officers and agents representing 230 separate agencies.

Scan this QR code with your smartphone to access related videos and additional information, or visit www.fbi.gov/occvii.

Left: Pirated software like this could be laced with malicious software, or malware.

Consumer Alert
Pirated Software May Contain Malware

You decide to order some software from an unknown online seller. The price is so low you just can't pass it up. What could go wrong?

Plenty. Whether you're downloading it or buying a physical disc, the odds are good that the product is pirated and laced with malicious software, or malware.

Today, the National Intellectual Property Rights Coordination (IPR) Center—of which the FBI is a key partner—is warning the American people about the real possibility that illegally copied software, including counterfeit products made to look authentic, could contain malware.

Our collective experience has shown this to be true, both through the complaints we've received and through our investigations. It's also been validated by industry studies, which show that an increasing amount of software installed on computers around the world—including in the U.S.—is pirated and that this software often contains malware.

As in our above scenario, pirated software can be obtained from unknown sellers and even from peer-to-peer networks. The physical discs can be purchased from online auction sites, less-than-reputable websites, and sometimes from street vendors and kiosks. Pirated software can also be found pre-installed on computers overseas, which are ordered by consumers online and then shipped into the United States.

Who's behind this crime? Criminals, hackers and hacker groups, and even organized crime rings.

And the risks to unsuspecting consumers? For starters, the inferior and infected software may not work properly. Your operating system may slow down and fail to receive critical security updates.

But the greater danger comes from potential exposure to criminal activity—like identity theft and financial fraud—after malware takes hold of your system.

Some very real dangers:

- Once installed on a computer, malware can record your keystrokes (capturing sensitive usernames and passwords) and steal your personally identifiable information (including Social Security numbers and birthdates), sending it straight back to criminals and hackers. It can also corrupt the data on your computer and even turn on your webcam and/or microphone.

- Malware can spread to other computers through removable media like thumb drives and through e-mails you send to your family, friends, and professional contacts. It can be spread through shared connections to a home, business, or even government network. Criminals can also use infected computers to launch attacks against other computers or against websites via denial of service attacks.

To guard against malware and other threats, read our tips on how to protect your computer at www.fbi.gov/scams-safety. If you think you may have purchased pirated software, or if you have information about sellers of pirated software, submit a tip to the IPR Center or the Internet Crime Complaint Center.

And know this: Pirated software is just one of the many threats that the IPR Center and the FBI are combating every year. The theft of U.S. intellectual property—the creative genius of the American people as expressed through everything from proprietary products and trade secrets to movies and music—takes a terrible toll on the nation. It poses significant (and sometimes life-threatening) risks to ordinary consumers, robs businesses of billions of dollars, and takes away jobs and tax revenue.

Learn more by visiting the IPR Center website at www.iprcenter.gov and the FBI's intellectual property theft webpage at www.fbi.gov/ipr.

Election Hack
Stealing Votes the Cyber Way

A 22-year-old candidate for student council president at California State University San Marcos hoped to guarantee victory by rigging the election through cyber fraud, but he ended up winning a year in prison instead.

Matthew Weaver used small electronic devices called keyloggers to steal the passwords and identities of nearly 750 fellow students. Then he cast votes for himself—and some of his friends on the ballot—using the stolen names. He was caught during the final hour of the election in March 2012, when network administrators noticed unusual voting activity associated with a single computer on campus. A Cal State police officer sent to investigate found Weaver working at that machine. He had cast more than 600 votes for himself using the stolen identities.

"Some people wanted to paint this as a college prank gone bad, but he took the identities of almost 750 people, and that's a serious thing," said Special Agent Charles Chabalko, who worked the investigation out of our San Diego Division after being contacted by Cal State authorities. "He had access to these students' e-mails, financial information, and their social networks. He had access to everything."

Weaver installed keyloggers—inexpensive devices easily purchased on the Internet—on 19 different campus computers. Those who used the machines were unaware that Weaver could later retrieve every keystroke they made, enabling him to obtain their usernames and passwords and then gain access to all their information.

When cyber investigator Chabalko and his partner, Special Agent Nick Arico, analyzed Weaver's laptop after his arrest, they found a spreadsheet that included the names of all the people whose identities he had stolen. "He kept a detailed accounting," Chabalko said.

And that's not all investigators found. Weaver had made online searches that included topics such as "jail time for keylogger" and "how to rig an election."

"He knew what he did was wrong," Chabalko said. "And even after he was caught, he didn't want to own up to what he did. He tried to cover up his actions and blame his crime on other students."

The evidence against Weaver was overwhelming, however, and he pled guilty in March 2013 to identity

theft, wire fraud, and unauthorized access of a computer. At his sentencing last month, the federal judge who sent Weaver to prison noted that Weaver trying to frame others for his crime is "the phenomenal misjudgment I just can't get around. That's what bothers me more than the original rigging of the election."

The investigators agreed, noting that while it was wrong for Weaver to try and steal the election, "what we were really concerned about was the privacy of those students whose identities he stole," Chabalko said. Prosecutors from the U.S. Attorney's Office felt the same way, writing in their sentencing memorandum, "Weaver determinedly and repeatedly spied on his classmates, stole their passwords, read their secrets, and usurped their votes—and he did it with his eyes wide open."

Weaver has a restitution hearing set for August 12, at which time the judge will hear evidence regarding the losses incurred by his victims. While the court has yet to determine those losses, Weaver and his friends on the ballot would have collected $36,000 in stipends and controlled a student budget of $300,000 if his vote-rigging plan had succeeded.

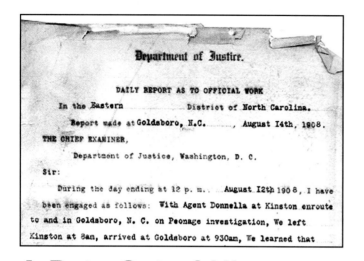

Left: A copy of a 1908 report prepared by Samuel Allred, one of our first agents.

A Byte Out of History
Civil Rights Case
One of Our First

The new special agent force announced by Attorney General Charles Bonaparte on July 26, 1908—the forerunner of today's FBI—was just days old when a civil rights crime in North Carolina led to one of its first investigations.

In the early morning hours of August 3, an African-American laborer named Arthur Dixon was arrested in Goldsboro for owing a debt of $4.20. Later that morning, he was tied with a rope and carried off to a nearby town to begin paying off his debt through forced labor.

It was a case of peonage—compelling a person to work to repay money owed. A fundamental denial of freedom without due process—and a practice that sometimes trapped people in a form of slavery when debts were never allowed to be fully repaid—peonage became a federal crime in 1867. Although rare in the late 1800s, peonage had become a regular practice in certain industries and parts of America by the early 20th century, and the Department of Justice was routinely investigating such cases.

Upon learning of the crime, two of our first agents—Samuel Nelson Allred and Schuyler A. Donnella—began investigating. They spoke first to Dixon's brother-in-law, a man named A. Wills, who was renting Dixon a room in his house. He said the pair was awakened at 3 a.m. by a police officer named High Ward, a constable of Rose Hill named Asa Fussell, and another man. Dixon was told he was under arrest for a debt owed to J.H. Fussell, whose family was prominent in local business and politics in Rose Hill. Wills told the agents that Constable Fussell

was a son of the man that had Dixon arrested.

For the next week, Allred and Donnella traveled to Rose Hill and surrounding areas by train, horse, buggy, and even on foot, interviewing potential witnesses. With enough evidence gathered, they met with the U.S. district attorney in Greenville, who issued warrants for the arrest of the Fussells on a charge of peonage. The father and son were apprehended by a deputy U.S. marshal (Bureau agents were not authorized to make arrests at that time) and later released on $1,000 bond. Prior to the grand jury hearing in November, Allred and Donnella canvassed potential witnesses, especially Wills and Dixon, to make sure they were available for the hearing in Raleigh. The agents' work was successful—on November 27, the jury indicted the two Fussells and a third man.

The matter was placed on the court's docket for May of the following year. What happened after that is unknown. If it was like many cases of that time, the Fussells probably pled guilty, paid a fine, and were given a short sentence that was then suspended. It's also possible the two were acquitted; peonage was so accepted in the day that juries in many areas would not convict even in the most horrendous cases.

Samuel N. Allred

The young Bureau's focus on peonage was short lived. Although it didn't disappear as a criminal violation, subsequent court rulings made certain types of peonage hard to prove. Other legal, social, and economic measures sapped the strength of civil rights protections for black Americans. Bureau agents experienced such investigative frustrations for many years, but five decades ago in the 1960s, the tide began to turn. Stay tuned for more stories on that subject in the months to come.

Seeking the Public's Assistance
New Information Released in Serial Killer Case

After Israel Keyes was arrested for the murder of 18-year-old Samantha Koenig in Alaska in 2012, authorities realized that the man they had in custody was a prolific serial killer. Keyes freely admitted as much.

During conversations with investigators, the 34-year-old sometime construction worker revealed the names of two additional victims—along with tantalizing clues about other murders he had committed around the country over a period of years. But last December, Keyes killed himself in his Anchorage jail cell, leaving a trail of unanswered questions and unidentified victims.

Those victims have not been forgotten, however. Today we are releasing new information in the hopes that the public can help us identify others who died by Keyes' hands. The information includes extensive videotaped conversations with Keyes in jail and an interactive map that contains a detailed timeline of his known movements beginning in 1997.

"He gave us a number of clues," said Special Agent Jolene Goeden in our Anchorage Division. "He talked openly about some of the homicides, but much of what he said only hinted at the things he had done. So we are trying to get information out there about what he did tell us. We are letting the public know the types of cars he rented, towns he visited, campgrounds he frequented. Anything that might spur someone's memory could help us," Goeden said.

Apart from Koenig, who was abducted from the Anchorage coffee stand where she worked, and Bill and Lorraine Currier, a middle-aged married couple who were murdered in 2011 in Vermont, Keyes discussed "seven or eight other victims," Goeden said. "We want to identify them."

Investigators believe that Keyes killed and buried a victim in upstate New York in April 2009. "He also told us about a couple in Washington state, another victim in that area, and possibly others in surrounding states," Goeden said.

FBI agents are working with law enforcement around the country to link Keyes to open cases. "If we have a missing person identified in a particular area, we work closely with that local police department to either

Suspected serial killer Israel Keyes

connect the person to Keyes or not," Goeden explained. "We have his DNA."

It's a painstaking process, made more complicated because Keyes was meticulous about covering his tracks. In the Currier case, for example, he flew from Alaska to Chicago, rented a car, and drove 1,000 miles to Vermont, where he searched for victims. He chose the Curriers at random.

Keyes also left "murder kits" in various locations around the country that contained, among other items, weapons and cash—the money came from bank robberies he committed to support his criminal activities. The caches provided further cover because Keyes didn't have to risk boarding an airplane with a weapon or using credit cards that could later connect him to a crime in a particular area.

"Although he chose many of his victims randomly, a tremendous amount of planning went into these crimes," Goeden said. "Keyes enjoyed what he did, and he had no remorse at all. He told us if he hadn't been caught, he would have continued kidnapping and murdering people."

We need your help. If you have any information regarding Keyes, please contact your local FBI office or submit a tip online.

"That fact that Keyes is dead makes it more difficult for us," Goeden said, "but the investigation absolutely continues."

Scan this QR code with your smartphone to access related videos, photos, audio clips, and timeline, or visit www.fbi.gov/israelkeyes.

Coin Crime
The Case of the Parking Meter Thief

A longtime employee of the city of Buffalo, New York was sentenced to 30 months in jail today for stealing more than $200,000—all in quarters—from the city's parking meters over a period of eight years.

James Bagarozzo, who had been employed by the city for more than three decades, became a parking meter mechanic in 2003—but instead of repairing the meters, he and an accomplice rigged more than 75 of them so he could steal quarters. Over time, his small-change crime added up.

"When he went to work," said Special Agent Rob Gross, who investigated the case out of our Buffalo Division, "half of his day was spent stealing from the city." After Bagarozzo and fellow city employee Lawrence Charles were arrested in December 2011, investigators found some $47,000 in cash and quarters in Bagarozzo's home, including $40,000 hidden in his bedroom ceiling.

As a parking meter mechanic, Bagarozzo was supposed to service and repair the city's 1,200 mechanical meters, but he didn't have access to their coin canisters and was not authorized to collect money. Instead, he rigged the meters so that deposited quarters never dropped into the coin canisters. Then he retrieved the money for himself.

Beginning in 2003 and continuing until the time of his arrest years later, the 57-year-old stole thousands upon thousands of quarters, using bags in his car or his deep-pocketed work pants to transfer the loot to his home, where he rolled the change in coin wrappers and exchanged it for cash at the bank.

"The bank never suspected," Gross said, "because Bagarozzo told the tellers he had a friend with a vending machine business. He developed such a good relationship with the bank tellers," Gross explained, "that they eventually gave him boxes to use that held exactly $500 worth of quarters. He went to the bank several times a week with a $500 box of quarters and got cash in return."

The scam might have continued indefinitely if not for the appointment of a new parking commissioner, who noticed a significant difference in revenue between the city's mechanical meters and newer electronic machines. In September 2010, the city's Division of Parking Enforcement began an investigation that expanded to include the Buffalo Police Department, and eventually the local authorities asked the FBI for assistance.

Bagarozzo and Charles—who is scheduled to be sentenced in two weeks—were caught on video committing the thefts on a daily basis. "Unless you were really paying attention," Gross said, "it looked like they were fixing the meters. In reality, they were stealing from them."

In September 2012, Bagarozzo pled guilty to theft from programs receiving federal funds and agreed to pay restitution of $210,000. According to the U.S. attorney who prosecuted the case, Bagarozzo used the meter money to pay for personal and family expenses.

"This case is a classic example of how public corruption strikes at the heart of government's ability to serve its people," said Richard Frankel, acting special agent in charge of our Buffalo Division. "We are gratified to see justice served in this case," he said, adding that "the FBI remains vigilant against all forms of public corruption."

Legal Attaché Manila
Then and Now

In August 1961—52 years ago—Special Agent Robert B. Hawley reported to the new U.S. Embassy office building on Manila Bay to open a small legal attaché (or legat) office that would cover criminal and intelligence matters in the Philippines.

It was not the first time FBI agents had served in the Philippines, though. In 1939, the Bureau had considered opening a regular domestic resident agency there, as the Philippines was still technically part of the United States. But it wasn't until March 1, 1945—two days shy of finally wresting Manila from Japanese troops—that General Douglas MacArthur invited an FBI liaison agent to serve there with General Thorpe's Army Counter Intelligence Corps. Special Agent Fred Tillman, a Japanese specialist, arrived in a city almost completely destroyed by bombs. His job: to work with the Corps' internal security section on postwar Japanese and related matters. He was installed in the Uy Su Bin Building on Quintin Paredes Street, given access to a Women's Army Corps steno and a Jeep, and set to work. Six months later, he left with Generals MacArthur and Thorpe for Tokyo, ultimately participating in the Pearl Harbor hearings in Washington and testifying at the "Tokyo Rose" trial in San Francisco. His colleague, Special Agent Nicolas Alaga, closed the Manila office in 1946.

By the time Bob Hawley arrived 15 years later, Manila had been transformed—booming, rebuilt, and once again known as a "Pearl of the Orient." He was responsible for police liaison in the Philippines, Singapore, and Thailand—then the Federation of Malaya and South Vietnam, too. It was a huge territory. Crime was on the rise, as were anti-American sentiments across Asia. Hundreds of U.S. fugitives needed to be tracked down, and communist-led intelligence operations against the United States proliferated. Hawley worked closely in all these areas with the Philippine National Bureau of Investigation under the leadership of Jose Lukban, then Jolly Bugarin, effectively building the foundation for wider, deeper, and more productive relationships with the full suite of today's Filipino law enforcement and intelligence agencies.

Twice since then, Legat Manila has been closed in response to government economy measures, then reopened to respond to new threats—most recently in 1988 with the rise of terrorism, the illegal drug trade, fugitive matters, and international organized crime. And

In 1961, Robert B. Hawley opened the first FBI legal attaché in Manila in rooms 416 and 418 of the U.S. Embassy office building. In 1962, Hawley moved the office next door (left rear) to the old U.S. High Commissioner's residence, converted to the Chancery. Manila Bay is in the background.

in 1995, the Philippine National Police uncovered bomb and terrorist plots in Manila by terrorist Ramzi Yousef and worked with us to bring him to justice.

Today, Legat Gib Wilson runs a complex operation from the second floor of the Chancery on Roxas Boulevard, in the very office that Bob Hawley built out. Beyond working with Philippine authorities on fugitive and terrorism cases, the office focuses on human trafficking issues, child sex tourism, and cyber crimes. Last year, with the superb support of its Filipino colleagues, Legat Manila returned 37 fugitives to the U.S. through deportation, renditions, and extraditions. Still at large in the area of terrorism alone: several extremist leaders wanted by the FBI via the Rewards for Justice program, including Abdul Basit Usman, Khair Mundos, and Zulkarnaen. Three are also on the FBI's Most Wanted Terrorist list: Raddulan Sahiron and Isnilon Totoni Hapilon of the Abu Sayyef Group and Zulkifli Abdhir of al Qaeda affiliate Jemaah Islamiya. Please let us know if you can provide any information that would help us find them.

WANTED BY THE FBI

The "Loan Ranger Bandit"
Unknown Serial Bank Robber

Serial Bank Robber
Help Us Catch the Loan Ranger Bandit

Over the past four years, a man authorities have dubbed the Loan Ranger Bandit has committed at least a dozen armed robberies of banks and other financial institutions in four different states—and he is so brazen he doesn't bother covering his face.

"We have a lot of good surveillance photos where he is looking directly at the camera," said Special Agent Russell Di Lisi, who is coordinating the investigation from our Dallas Division. "Somebody out there has to know him or recognize him, and that's why we need the public's help."

A reward of up to $10,000 is being offered for information leading to the identification, arrest, and conviction of the Loan Ranger Bandit. Beginning in 2009, he has robbed banks in Arkansas, Mississippi, Kentucky, and Texas. His most recent robbery was last month in Temple, Texas at the Santa Fe Community Credit Union—the second time he has targeted that institution.

"He is a lot more reckless now," said Di Lisi, explaining that in the early robberies, the bandit would give tellers a demand note and show them a weapon in his waistband. "Beginning with the ninth robbery and every one since then," Di Lisi said, "he has actually brandished the weapon."

Officials with the Tyler Police Department in Texas came up with the Loan Ranger Bandit's moniker because the robber is known to target financial institutions that make loans, and he wore a Texas Rangers baseball cap in one of his first robberies.

"He usually wears different hats," Di Lisi said, "but he makes no effort to cover his face." Di Lisi noted that despite his lack of a disguise, the Loan Ranger Bandit is clever. He picks stand-alone institutions that offer easy access to major roadways—and therefore quick getaways—and he often targets the same banks more than once. "He's very confident in what he's doing," Di Lisi said. "I believe he's going to keep hitting banks until we catch him."

The bandit is described as a white male in his early 30s, approximately 5'7" inches to 6' tall, about 200 pounds, with a medium build. He has short, light brown hair, wears glasses, and has a small mole or mark just above his right eye on the lower part of his forehead. His varied clothing styles have included athletic wear, jeans, and business attire. He may also drive a maroon Chevrolet S-10 pickup truck with a white pinstripe around the truck bed. He should be considered armed and dangerous and should not be approached.

More information about the Loan Ranger Bandit, along with a number of detailed surveillance pictures, can be viewed on bankrobbers.fbi.gov, the Bureau's national website that features wanted bank robbers.

We need your help: If you have any information about the Loan Ranger Bandit, contact your local FBI office, submit a tip online, or call 1-800-CALL-FBI. Any information, even if it seems small, may be the connection we need to solve these crimes—and make you eligible for the $10,000 reward.

"It's been almost four years, and he's still out there," Di Lisi said. "With the public's help, we need to catch this guy before he strikes again."

Note: The Loan Ranger bandit may have been located since the above information was posted on our website. Please check our Wanted Bank Robbers website at bankrobbers.fbi. gov for up-to-date information.

Scamming Nuns
Con Artist Gets His Due

There's no limit to how low con artists will go to swindle victims out of their money—often targeting the elderly, the terminally ill, homeowners on the brink of losing their homes, even the lonely looking for companionship online.

Here's another category of victims to add to that list: members of religious communities who spend their lives tending to the sick and the poor.

Earlier this month, a New Jersey man was sentenced to 18 years in prison for defrauding members of the Puerto Rico-based Dominican Sisters of the Rosary of Fatima and others of more than a million dollars. He was also ordered to pay $1 million in restitution to his victims.

The scheme began back in 2009, when Adriano Sotomayor—born in Puerto Rico—obtained names and telephone numbers of certain Roman Catholic nuns and priests on the island…including an elderly nun from the Sisters of Fatima. Claiming to be a New Jersey priest, he called and said a deceased member of his parish community had named her the beneficiary of a $2.1 million estate. Sotomayor also told the nun that before receiving her funds, she had to wire money to the company handling the will—a New Jersey-based business called Flex Account—to cover various taxes, processing, and legal fees.

Of course, none of it was true. There was no deceased parishioner, no will, and no company called Flex Account. It was simply a con man working an angle. Unfortunately, it was believable enough to the nun, and the Sisters of Fatima thought they could use the money from the will to develop a religious community in Haiti.

There was just one problem…the nun had little money of her own and couldn't afford all the advance fees. So she borrowed money from Sisters of Fatima members, family, and friends in Puerto Rico and Pennsylvania (where the sisters also had a presence), then wired the money—per Sotomayor's instructions—to various locations in the Atlantic City area. Many of the transfers went to casinos—Sotomayor was known to be a gambler—and were picked up by individuals working for him. And the nun gave the wiring instructions to her acquaintances willing to loan her money; they in turn sent their shares to those same places.

Turns out, it wasn't enough. Soon, Sotomayor began

telling the nun that there were problems with the will, including a legal challenge by the deceased's son, and additional money was needed to avoid lawsuits. He threatened her with media attention and law enforcement action if she didn't send more money.

In an effort to expand the scheme even further, Sotomayor contacted individuals who had already wired money on behalf of the nun and told them if they sent additional money, they could get a portion of the will proceeds themselves.

But eventually the FBI—after receiving a complaint about a possible fraud scheme victimizing nuns and others—was able to uncover the breadth of the scheme and identified Adriano Sotomayor as the man behind it. Though he fled the day after being indicted, the FBI captured him in Las Vegas.

The most important lesson to be learned from this case? Do your homework before parting with your hard-earned money.

Left: Director Robert S. Mueller, III in his office at FBI Headquarters.

End of an Era
Robert S. Mueller Set to Step Down as FBI Director

Robert S. Mueller arrived at the FBI on September 4, 2001, one week before the terror attacks that shook the nation and the world. Twelve years later, the longest-serving Director since J. Edgar Hoover is widely credited with transforming the organization while maintaining the bedrock ideals that have been the FBI's hallmark for more than a century: fidelity, bravery, and integrity.

"When I first came on board, I thought I had a fair idea of what to expect," Mueller said recently during a farewell ceremony at FBI Headquarters to honor his tenure as Director. "But the September 11 attacks altered every expectation."

Mueller, who will step down as Director next week, reshaped the Bureau from a traditional law enforcement agency to a threat-focused, intelligence-based national security organization, said FBI Deputy Director Sean Joyce. "He guided the FBI through a period of tremendous change."

At the ceremony attended by employees, incoming Director James Comey, and former FBI Directors William Webster, William Sessions, and Louis Freeh, Joyce noted that Mueller has served the American people for four decades—as a decorated Marine, a prosecutor and former U.S. attorney, and leader of the FBI.

"As a prosecutor," Mueller said, "I had worked closely with the FBI over the years. But I had not witnessed firsthand the FBI's incredible response in times of crisis or the ability of the Bureau's men and women to band together to do what is needed—without fanfare or drama—and with a level of efficiency and excellence that is unrivaled."

As FBI Director for 12 years—he agreed to extend his 10-year term at the request of President Obama—Mueller faced the daunting task of keeping the country safe from terror attacks while maintaining the Bureau's established crime-fighting role. "People talk about change in the Bureau," he said, "but I consider what we were doing as augmenting the traditional capabilities the FBI already possessed."

Mueller said he still worries about the threat of terrorism—international and domestic—and cyber crime is a growing danger to our national security. "Should a terrorist utilize cyber capabilities to undertake an attack, it could be devastating," he said. "We have to be prepared."

The American people expect the FBI to be vigilant against such attacks while continuing to put corrupt politicians in jail, arrest violent criminals and scam artists, and keep the country's secrets safe from spies. "Those are substantial responsibilities, and we are up to the task," Mueller said, "but we need the support and the funding to exercise our capabilities."

During his tenure as Director, Mueller regularly spoke of the "FBI family" and the Bureau's responsibility to help keep the nation safe. "We have unique mission and a unique legacy that has been passed down to us," he said. "People in the FBI are tremendously proud to be a part of that legacy." For more than a century, he added, "the FBI has stood for the best of America. And we have done this by adhering to our motto of fidelity, bravery, and integrity. … It has been my greatest honor and privilege to have been part of the FBI family for the past 12 years."

Scan this **QR code** with your smartphone to access related video and photos, or visit www.fbi.gov/muellertenure.

The Crime of 'Swatting'
Fake 9-1-1 Calls Have Real Consequences

The distraught-sounding man told the 9-1-1 operator he shot a family member and might kill others in the house. A SWAT team was urgently dispatched to the address corresponding to the caller's phone number. But when the tactical team arrived, ready for a possible violent encounter, they found only a surprised family panicked by the officers at their door.

It's called "swatting"—making a hoax call to 9-1-1 to draw a response from law enforcement, usually a SWAT team. The individuals who engage in this activity use technology to make it appear that the emergency call is coming from the victim's phone. Sometimes swatting is done for revenge, sometimes as a prank. Either way, it is a serious crime, and one that has potentially dangerous consequences.

Since we first warned about this phone hacking phenomenon in 2008, the FBI has arrested numerous individuals on federal charges stemming from swatting incidents, and some are currently in prison. Today, although most swatting cases are handled by local and state law enforcement agencies, the Bureau often provides resources and guidance in these investigations.

"The FBI looks at these crimes as a public safety issue," said Kevin Kolbye, an assistant special agent in charge in our Dallas Division. "It's only a matter of time before somebody gets seriously injured as a result of one of these incidents."

There have already been close calls. A police officer was injured in a car accident during an emergency response that turned out to be a swatting incident, Kolbye said, and some unsuspecting victims—caught off guard when SWAT teams suddenly arrived on their doorsteps—have suffered mild heart attacks.

"The victims are scared and taken by surprise," he said. Law enforcement personnel, meanwhile, rush to the scene of a swatting incident on high alert. "They believe they have a violent subject to apprehend or an innocent victim to rescue," Kolbye explained. "It's a dangerous situation any way you look at it."

It is also expensive. It can cost thousands of dollars every time a SWAT team is called out. And although there are no national statistics on how many swatting incidents

"Swatting" is a prank designed to draw a law enforcement response to a hoax victim.

occur annually, Kolbye guesses there are hundreds. A recent trend, he said, is so-called celebrity swatting, where the targeted victims are well-known actors and musicians.

"People who make these swatting calls are very credible," he said. "They have no trouble convincing 9-1-1 operators they are telling the truth." And thanks to "spoofing" technology—which enables callers to mask their own numbers while making the victims' numbers appear—emergency operators are doubly tricked.

Most who engage in swatting are serial offenders also involved in other cyber crimes such as identity theft and credit card fraud, Kolbye said. They either want to brag about their swatting exploits or exact revenge on someone who angered them online.

Kolbye suggests making a police report about any swatting threats you receive online. Such threats typically come from the online gaming community, where competitors can play and interact anonymously. With a report on file, if a 9-1-1 incident does occur at your home, the police will be aware that it could be a hoax.

"The FBI takes swatting very seriously," Kolbye said. "Working closely with industry and law enforcement partners, we continue to refine our technological capabilities and our investigative techniques to stop the thoughtless individuals who commit these crimes. The bottom line," he added, "is that swatting puts innocent people at risk."

Transnational Law Enforcement Efforts
Helping Stem Transnational Crime

Four leaders of the MS-13 gang were convicted in Atlanta recently in connection with a terrorizing violent crime spree. During the course of the investigation, we determined that many of their violent acts were directed by gang leadership in El Salvador and Honduras—a common occurrence uncovered in other investigations as well. This international criminal nexus of violent gangs is the focus of several FBI programs funded by the U.S. State Department through the Central American Regional Security Initiative (CARSI).

CARSI's goal is to confront the dangers of organized crime, violent gangs, and drug trafficking in Central America and the U.S., and several domestic federal agencies participate in various facets of the initiative. The FBI, through its National Gang Task Force (NGTF), specifically supports six programs targeting the transnational threats posed by the MS-13 and 18th Street gangs.

The first three are operationally focused:

Transnational Anti-Gang (TAG) Unit: This program combines the expertise, resources, and jurisdiction of participating agencies involved in investigating and countering transnational criminal gang activity in the U.S. and Central America. These groups—headed by FBI agents who lead vetted teams of national police and prosecutors in El Salvador, Guatemala, and Honduras—coordinate with FBI legal attachés assigned to those regions and with the Bureau's International Operations Division.

Central American Fingerprint Exchange (CAFÉ): This NGTF-established program was developed to collect and store criminal biometric data, including fingerprint records, from all Central American countries. The collected prints are added to the FBI's Criminal Justice Information Services Division's general database, where they're accessible to local, state, and federal agencies in the U.S.

Criminal History Information Program (CHIP): Through this initiative, the FBI provides the Salvadoran and Honduran National Police with the criminal history, biographical, and background information of non-U.S. citizen gang members and associates who are deported from the U.S. back to their home countries.

The second three CARSI programs are more training-focused:

Central American Law Enforcement Exchange (CALEE): This officer exchange program provides Central American and U.S. police officers with hands-on training that emphasizes operational techniques and current gang trends. CALEE encourages relationship-building and innovative approaches for gang investigations and offers a clearer understanding of the transnational threat posed by violent criminal street gangs. This four-week program takes part in classrooms and in the field.

Central American Intelligence Program (CAIP): CAIP allows representatives from U.S. and Central American law enforcement agencies to take part in an interactive, custom-designed intelligence and exchange program. CAIP was developed to expose participants to best practices in the areas of collection, analysis, and dissemination of transnational gang intelligence.

Central American Community Impact Exchange (CACIE): With its goal of helping Central American nations develop positive community impact programs, CACIE focuses on the importance of community collaboration and strengthening relationships between community leaders and law enforcement. The newest of the CARSI programs, CACIE was developed in partnership with the State Department and the White House national security staff.

These six CARSI programs have proven to be a valuable weapon against transnational gangs and have assisted the FBI and our partners in targeting and disrupting many MS-13 and 18th Street gang connections—proof positive that transnational cooperation among law enforcement can trump cross-border collaboration among criminals.

Serial Killers
Part 1: The FBI's Role Takes Shape

Seventeen years ago yesterday—on September 9, 1996—a teenager disappeared from her home in Spotsylvania County, Virginia. Tragically, she was found dead the following month. The next May, two sisters in the same county went missing after coming home from school. Five days later, their bodies were found in a river about 40 miles away.

This trio of murders was the work of a serial killer named Richard Marc Evonitz. It took another five years for him to be identified. In June 2002, after a teenage girl managed to escape from a kidnapper in South Carolina, she identified Evonitz as her abductor. He fled to Florida and committed suicide as authorities closed in. Valuable trace evidence collected by the FBI later definitively linked him to the murders of the three Virginia girls. He is suspected of more homicides and other attacks.

Although relatively rare, serial killings have both horrified and fascinated the American people for decades. Serial murderers have existed throughout history and have been popularized by such killers as Jack the Ripper in England and Herman Webster Mudgett in the United States in the late 1800s. The exact origin of the term serial killer or serial murderer is not known, but it appears to have come into use in law enforcement circles in the 1970s and more commonly in society in the 1980s and 1990s.

Over the years, the FBI has played a slowly evolving role in addressing the threat of serial killers. In its earliest days, few violent crimes fell under the Bureau's jurisdiction. It depended on where the crime occurred—if it was on government property, the high seas, or certain Indian reservations, the FBI took charge. In the 1930s, the FBI became a household name as it tackled violent gangsters and gained more law enforcement authorities in the process. In the 1950s and '60s, the Bureau supported local and state law enforcement in some high-profile serial killer cases like the Boston Strangler and the Zodiac Killer of Northern California.

It was in the 1970s, however, that the FBI's role in addressing serial killers began to grow as new capabilities were developed. Building on earlier work in New York and elsewhere, Special Agent Howard Teten and others in the Bureau began to apply the insights of

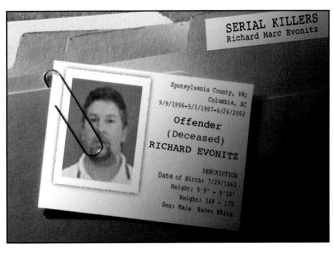

Richard Marc Evonitz committed three murders in Virginia. Over the years, the FBI has played a slowly evolving role in addressing the threat of serial killers.

psychology and behavioral science to violent criminal behavior in a comprehensive way. Since then, the FBI has become a leader in behavioral analysis, providing an array of support and training to help identify serial killers and to prevent future violence.

The FBI's involvement in serial killer cases has also evolved under federal law. For example, the Bureau was authorized to investigate violent crimes against interstate travelers in 1994 and serial killings specifically in 1998. The FBI may investigate only when requested to do so by an appropriate law enforcement agency. The Bureau is also authorized to provide a variety of support services, from laboratory and behavioral analysis to crime statistics collection and the sharing of criminal identification and history information through our longstanding services and systems.

In the coming months, FBI.gov will examine the Bureau's role in addressing serial killings in more detail, including our work in some of the most horrific serial murder investigations in the last 40 years.

Part 2: The birth of behavioral analysis in the FBI (page 77)

Left: Investigators at the 16th Street Baptist Church in Birmingham after it was bombed on September, 15, 1963.

Civil Rights in the '60s
Part 2: Retired Investigators Reflect on 16th Street Baptist Church Bombing

On September 15, 1963—50 years ago this Sunday—five young girls preparing for Sunday worship services were in the basement of the 16th Street Baptist Church in Birmingham, Alabama, when a bomb tore through the church's east wall, killing four of them.

The blast at the African-American church—a popular meeting place for civil rights leaders like the Rev. Martin Luther King, Jr.—was a turning point in the civil rights movement. The killing of young innocents— Addie Mae Collins, Denice McNair, Carole Robertson, and Cynthia Wesley—drew national attention to Birmingham…a city some already called "Bombingham" because of its pattern of racially motivated attacks.

The FBI sent dozens of agents to investigate, but reluctant witnesses and a lack of prosecutable evidence made it hard to bring the bombers to justice. It wasn't until a decade later in 1977 that one of the bombers, Robert "Dynamite" Chambliss, was convicted for his role in the case, but evidence still suggested more conspirators. In the mid-'90s FBI Birmingham Special Agent in Charge Rob Langford reopened the case, assigning senior agent Bill Fleming and recruiting Birmingham Police Department Sgt. Ben Herren to work it full time.

"It pretty much looked like an uphill battle," said Herren, who is now retired and living in Birmingham. He and Fleming were initially reluctant to take the case, given that more than 100 potential witnesses had died in the decades since the bombing. In 1996, Herren recalled

thinking it was the ultimate cold case. "But if we're going to do it," he said at the time, "we need to do it right, because this is the last time that it would be feasible to try to reinvestigate."

For nearly 15 months, the two scoured the case files with a singular focus on finding new leads. "I didn't read anything else about it," Herren said. "I wanted the files to lead me through the investigation instead of me trying to lead the investigation." The files led them back to familiar names from earlier probes.

They tracked down Bobby Cherry, a known Birmingham Ku Klux Klan member who had moved to Texas, and interviewed him for four hours. The exchange so incensed Cherry that he called a press conference to loudly proclaim his innocence. It made national news, and the FBI's phones started ringing. "This was the best thing to happen to our investigation," Fleming said, "because we started getting witnesses and people that were able to give us information." The witness accounts would eventually implicate Cherry at trial.

As tips rolled in and more witnesses stepped forward, Fleming and Herren expanded their focus to Tommy Blanton, who was suspected in the early investigation— enough so that agents had planted listening devices at his home. Fleming tracked down the old reel-to-reel tapes, which revealed Blanton explaining to his wife and another man the details of how the bomb plot unfolded.

Relying heavily on the tapes, a jury in 2001 needed only a couple hours to render a guilty verdict against Blanton on state murder charges. He was sentenced to life in prison, where he remains today. Cherry was convicted in 2002 for his role as a co-conspirator and sentenced to life in prison, where he died in 2004.

Fleming and Herren, who remain close friends today, have been lauded for their tireless work. But they are quick to credit others who stepped forward in the course of their investigation.

"If it was not for the people who read the paper and [saw] the TV spot—and all we had was the file—I don't know that we would have ever accomplished anything," Fleming said. Both have said the investigation was the most rewarding case they ever worked. "You feel like you have done the job," Herren said. "Even though it looked like a tremendous uphill battle, we finally got justice for the little girls."

Latest Crime Stats Released
Violent Crime Up, Property Crime Down

According to our just-released *Crime in the United States, 2012* report, the estimated number of violent crimes reported to law enforcement increased 0.7 percent over 2011 figures. And the estimated number of property crimes decreased 0.9 percent from 2011—the 10th year in a row that property crimes showed a decline.

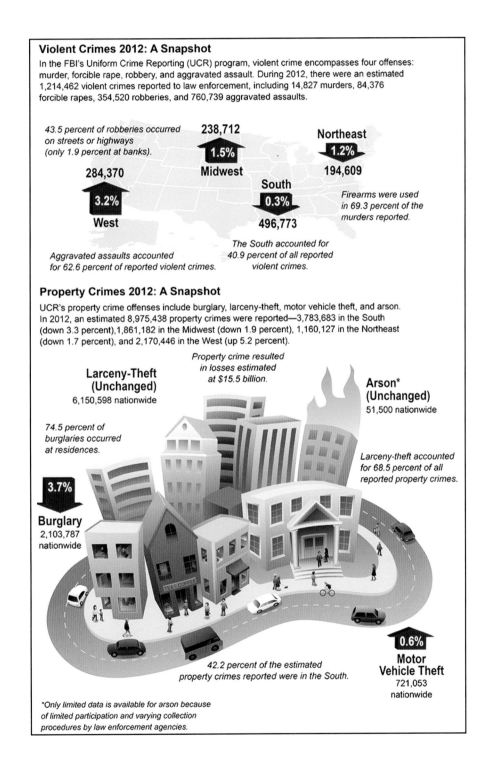

Violent Crimes 2012: A Snapshot

In the FBI's Uniform Crime Reporting (UCR) program, violent crime encompasses four offenses: murder, forcible rape, robbery, and aggravated assault. During 2012, there were an estimated 1,214,462 violent crimes reported to law enforcement, including 14,827 murders, 84,376 forcible rapes, 354,520 robberies, and 760,739 aggravated assaults.

43.5 percent of robberies occurred on streets or highways (only 1.9 percent at banks).

238,712
1.5%
Midwest

Northeast
1.2%
194,609

284,370
3.2%
West

South
0.3%
496,773

Firearms were used in 69.3 percent of the murders reported.

Aggravated assaults accounted for 62.6 percent of reported violent crimes.

The South accounted for 40.9 percent of all reported violent crimes.

Property Crimes 2012: A Snapshot

UCR's property crime offenses include burglary, larceny-theft, motor vehicle theft, and arson. In 2012, an estimated 8,975,438 property crimes were reported—3,783,683 in the South (down 3.3 percent), 1,861,182 in the Midwest (down 1.9 percent), 1,160,127 in the Northeast (down 1.7 percent), and 2,170,446 in the West (up 5.2 percent).

Property crime resulted in losses estimated at $15.5 billion.

Larceny-Theft (Unchanged)
6,150,598 nationwide

Arson* (Unchanged)
51,500 nationwide

74.5 percent of burglaries occurred at residences.

Larceny-theft accounted for 68.5 percent of all reported property crimes.

3.7%
Burglary
2,103,787 nationwide

0.6%
Motor Vehicle Theft
721,053 nationwide

42.2 percent of the estimated property crimes reported were in the South.

*Only limited data is available for arson because of limited participation and varying collection procedures by law enforcement agencies.

Public Corruption: Courtroom for Sale
Judge Gets Jail Time in Racketeering Case

In a case that exposed widespread corruption in a South Texas county's judicial system—reaching all the way to the district attorney's office—a former state judge was recently sentenced to six years in prison for taking bribes and kickbacks in return for favorable rulings from his bench.

Abel Limas, 59, a lifelong resident of Brownsville, Texas, served as a police officer and practiced law before becoming a state judge in Cameron County in 2001. He served eight years on the bench, during which time he turned his courtroom into a criminal enterprise to line his own pockets.

"The depth of the corruption was shocking," said Mark Gripka, a special agent in our San Antonio Division who was part of the team that investigated the case. "What was more shocking was how cheaply Judge Limas sold his courtroom—$300 here, $500 there—in return for a favorable ruling."

There was plenty of big money involved as well. Limas received more than $250,000 in bribes and kickbacks while he was on the bench. He took money from attorneys with civil cases pending in his court in return for favorable pre-trial rulings, most notably in a case involving a Texas helicopter crash that was later settled for $14 million. Referring to an $8,000 payment Limas received in that case, our investigators listened on the telephone as he described the cash to an accomplice as eight golf balls. "Their code language didn't fool anybody," Gripka said.

Evidence also showed that Limas made a deal with the attorneys in the helicopter crash case to become an "of counsel" attorney with the firm. He was promised an advance of $100,000 and 10 percent of the settlement—all while the case was still pending in his court.

Over a 14-month period beginning in November 2007, investigators used court-authorized wiretaps to listen to the judge's phone calls. "That's when we really learned the scope of what he was doing," Gripka explained. The judge's nearly $100,000 annual salary was not enough to support his lifestyle, which included regular gambling trips to Las Vegas.

In 2010, when Limas was faced with the overwhelming evidence against him, he began to cooperate in a wider public corruption investigation—and our agents learned that the Cameron County district attorney at the time, Armando Villalobos, was also corrupt. The investigation showed, among other criminal activities, that Villalobos accepted $80,000 in cash in exchange for taking actions that allowed a convicted murderer to be released for 60 days without bond prior to reporting to prison. The murderer failed to report to prison and remains a fugitive.

Limas pled guilty to racketeering in 2011. By that time, he had helped authorities uncover wide-ranging corruption in the Cameron County judicial system. To date, 10 other defendants have been convicted by a jury or pled guilty as part of the FBI's six-year investigation, including a former Texas state representative, three attorneys, a former investigator for the district attorney's office, and Villalobos, who is scheduled to be sentenced next month on racketeering, extortion, and bribery charges.

"During the course of this investigation, we interviewed over 800 people, including many local attorneys in Cameron County," Gripka said. "We hope this case shows everyone that the government will not tolerate officials who violate the public trust. Fighting public corruption is a priority for the FBI," he added, "and it is something we take very seriously."

New Internet Crime Initiative
Combines Resources, Expertise

A pilot program targeting Internet crime—focused on establishing a model for sharing information and coordinating investigations—was recently launched by the FBI's Internet Crime Complaint Center (IC3) and the state of Utah.

"The Utah pilot is the first step in our efforts to fix a gap that the FBI and our state and local law enforcement partners have recognized exists in the investigation and prosecution of Internet fraud," said Richard McFeely, executive assistant director of the Bureau's Criminal, Cyber, Response, and Services Branch. "Because not all Internet fraud schemes rise to the level necessary to prosecute them in federal court, we are enhancing how we package the investigative leads we receive at IC3 and disseminating those packages directly to state and local agencies." Based on the initial results of the Utah pilot, he said, the FBI plans to expand it to other states.

Internet fraud and other Internet-based crimes for profit cause untold financial losses each year. The IC3 reports that in 2012 alone, victims reported more than $500 million in losses due to crimes like fraudulent auto sales, intimidation/extortion scams, online dating fraud, scareware and ransomware, auction fraud, charity fraud, and computer intrusions. Our new initiative, led by IC3 with the assistance of our Cyber and Criminal Investigative Divisions, combines law enforcement resources to strategically pursue criminals responsible for these kinds of crimes.

How the program works. Using its complaint database and its analytical capabilities, IC3 personnel create actionable intelligence packages that are connected to particular geographic regions. These packages can highlight trends, identity individuals and criminal enterprises based on commonalities of complaints, link different methods of operation back to the same organization, and detect various layers of criminal activity. They will also contain results of preliminary investigative research performed by IC3 analysts, including criminal record checks and basic web domain searches.

Once the packages are complete, they are submitted to the local FBI cyber task force for further action, giving investigators a leg up on any case before the first interview is even conducted.

Our cyber task forces, located in every field office, are made up of FBI agents, other federal representatives, and state and local law enforcement dedicated to investigating a whole range of cyber threats, including Internet crime. In the Utah pilot program, our agents team up with officers from the Utah Department of Public Safety's Bureau of Investigation, along with federal and local prosecutors. Decisions are made jointly whether to prosecute locally or federally, or if violations of local statutes can be combined in a federal prosecution going after an entire criminal enterprise that operates across jurisdictional lines.

Another vital aspect of our focused effort to investigate Internet crime is partnering with state agencies charged with the regulatory policing of the various entities being investigated—like consumer protection bureaus—as well as federal regulatory agencies. Our cyber task force in Salt Lake City has made those partnerships a priority.

A note to the public: The information extracted from crime complaints submitted to IC3 is the bedrock of this initiative, so the more complaints IC3 receives, the more effective law enforcement can be in identifying and arresting those responsible. If you believe you or someone you know may have been a victim of Internet crime, please file a complaint with IC3.

Left: FBI Criminal Investigative Division Assistant Director Ronald Hosko discusses charges against nine auto parts makers during a press conference in Washington, D.C. At left is Deputy Assistant Attorney General Scott Hammond of DOJ's Antitrust Division.

Sticker Shock
Guilty Pleas Show High Cost of Price-Fixing in Auto Industry

Price-fixing conspiracies by auto parts manufacturers may have inflated the cost of your new car. In announcing guilty pleas by nine Japan-based auto parts makers and two executives, the Justice Department today laid out details of brazen collusion schemes to rig the prices of more than 30 kinds of car parts—like seat belts, radiators, and windshield wipers—sold to U.S. car makers.

The conspiracies—some lasting a decade or more— affected more than $5 billion in automotive parts and more than 25 million cars purchased by U.S. consumers.

"The scheme directly impacted your bank account," said FBI Criminal Investigative Division Assistant Director Ronald Hosko at a press conference today, where he was joined by Attorney General Eric Holder and Scott Hammond, head of the Criminal Enforcement Program in the Justice Department's Antitrust Division. "These individuals and companies drove up costs for both vehicle makers and buyers, which caused you to spend more."

Automakers affected include Ford, General Motors, and Chrysler, as well as the U.S. subsidiaries of Honda, Mazda, Mitsubishi, Nissan, Subaru, and Toyota. Auto plants in Detroit and 13 other states were victims. FBI agents in 11 field offices investigated the cases.

Charges filed in Detroit, Cincinnati, and Toledo reveal the lengths conspirators went to gain unfair advantage. In phone calls and secretive meetings—sometimes using code names—the companies agreed to rig bids, set prices, and manipulate the supply of parts to U.S. car makers.

Hammond said car makers—which already operate on tight margins—were victimized along with consumers. When car makers put out requests for bids, he said, "What they didn't realize is that in back rooms and secret meetings in the United States and Japan, their suppliers were getting together and allocating business and fixing the prices."

The guilty pleas announced Thursday bring to 20 the number of companies charged in the Justice Department's ongoing multi-year investigation of the auto industry. Seventeen of 21 executives have also been charged, with most of them facing or already serving prison time. Additionally, heavy fines have been imposed—more than $740 million since the investigation began in 2011. With the recent charges, criminal fines could reach $1.6 billion.

In one case, Gary Walker, an American executive with a Japanese company operating in Auburn Hills, Michigan, rigged bids between 2003 and 2010 to fix the prices of seat belts sold to Toyota, Nissan, Honda, and Mazda manufacturers, according to the federal charges. Other defendants—including Hitachi Automotive Systems Ltd., Mitsubishi Electric Corporation, and Jtekt Corporation— rigged bids on starter motors, alternators, ignition coils, bearings, and other essential vehicle components.

The FBI and Antitrust Division worked closely on the case with counterparts overseas, including the Japan Fair Trade Commission. Search warrants in the U.S. were coordinated with searches overseas.

Hosko said companies trying to game the system should note the stiff penalties meted out as a result of the investigation and prosecutions. "Today's events and the last few years of investigation should send a clear message to companies that suffer from the notion that they don't need to follow the rules," he said. "If you violate the laws of this country, the FBI and the Justice Department will investigate and stop the threat you pose to our economy and to hardworking Americans."

A Byte Out of History
The Bobby Greenlease Kidnapping

On September 28, 1953—60 years ago this past weekend—a woman knocked on the door of the French Institute of Notre Dame de Sion in Kansas City, Missouri. When a nun answered, the woman explained that she was the aunt of Bobby Greenlease, a 6-year-old student at the school, and that his mother had just suffered a heart attack and she needed to take the boy immediately. Except the woman was not Bobby's aunt, and his mother had not suffered a heart attack. Instead, Bonnie Emily Heady had just kidnapped the son of a very wealthy Kansas City car dealer.

It's every parent's worst nightmare...but what happened next was even worse. The plan, masterminded by Heady's paramour, Carl Austin Hall, was to extract a significant ransom from the worried parents—$600,000, to be exact—in exchange for the boy's safe return. But Hall and Heady never intended to carry out their end of the bargain. After driving Bobby away from the school, all the while chatting with him about his pets and even buying him ice cream, the trio continued on to a secluded farm in Kansas, where Hall, who considered the boy evidence that needed to be destroyed, shot Bobby at point-blank range, killing him.

That didn't stop Hall and Heady from cashing in. After nearly a week of 15 phone calls and more than a half-dozen ransom notes that sent the Greenlease family on a wild goose chase, the two eventually got their loot. Hall then promised to send instructions on where to pick up Bobby...instructions that, unlike the other notes, were never delivered.

It all seemed to go off without a hitch...until they picked up the ransom money on October 5 with no plans on what to do next. Hall and Heady, both severe alcoholics who couldn't start the day without a drink, drove nearly 380 miles to St. Louis and rented an apartment. When Heady passed out, Hall put $2,000 in her purse and left.

By enlisting the services of a cab driver, a prostitute, and copious amounts of alcohol, Hall may have been a bit too free with his newly acquired money—leading the cab driver to report his suspicious fare to the St. Louis Police Department. On October 6, officers arrested Hall. The FBI was notified and quickly tied him to the kidnapping. Hall gave up Heady, who was arrested the same night.

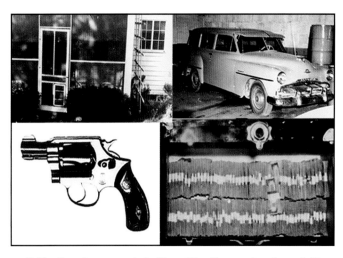

Bobby Greenlease was shot with a .38 caliber revolver (lower left) in his kidnappers' vehicle (top right) and buried in a shallow grave beneath a trellis on Bonnie Heady's property (top left). The boy's parents had paid Heady and Carl Hall a $600,000 ransom (lower right) for the 6-year-old boy's safe return.

The Bureau had been involved in the case from the beginning, and its extensive investigation not only led to the recovery of Robert Cosgrove Greenlease, Jr.'s body in a grave on Heady's property in St. Joseph, Missouri, but also resulted in dozens of pages of confessions and indisputable evidence. Hall and Heady were tried, convicted, and—after just over an hour of deliberation by the jury—sentenced to death for the crime. As Judge Albert L. Reeves said of the case, "I think the verdict fits the evidence. It is the most coldblooded, brutal murder I have ever tried."

On December 18, 1953—less than three months after Bobby's kidnapping—Hall and Heady were executed together in Missouri's gas chamber. The Greenlease family never got their beloved son back. But, thanks to the hard work of the FBI and its partners, justice was served.

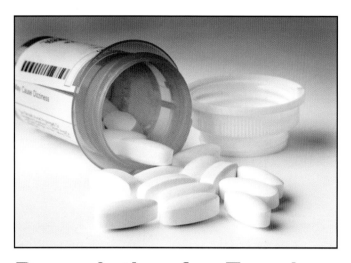

Prescription for Fraud
Internet Pharmacy Operator Gets Jail Time

A Florida man has been sentenced to prison for his role in importing cancer drugs manufactured overseas and then illegally selling them to doctors in the U.S.—and two doctors who bought the deeply discounted medicines have been held accountable as well.

Martin Paul Bean pled guilty to selling unapproved and misbranded drugs, conspiracy to commit wire fraud, mail fraud, and other federal violations and was sentenced recently to two years in prison.

Bean and an associate used a marketing technique known as "blast faxing" to target oncologists around the country. The one-page fax that arrived in hundreds of doctors' offices advertised generic cancer medicines at 20 to 35 percent discounts—and led doctors to believe that the drugs were approved by the Food and Drug Administration (FDA) as required by law.

In fact, the drugs—marketed in the U.S. as Gemzar7, Taxotere7, Eloxatin7, Zometa7, and Kytril7—were manufactured in Turkey, India, and Pakistan and were not approved by the FDA. The drugs were shipped from overseas to California, where they were repackaged and illegally sent to doctors in California, Florida, Texas, and elsewhere.

"Our investigation identified more than 50 doctors across the country who purchased the cancer drugs from Bean's online GlobalRX Store," said Special Agent Brad Godshall, who worked the case from our San Diego Division. "Ultimately, we were able to dismantle the entire operation."

Although many of the doctors who purchased the drugs were unaware of the fraud—some even became suspicious and notified authorities when they received shipments with foreign labeling—Godshall believes "many of the doctors who ordered from Bean didn't do the due diligence that their position required of them. They simply relied on the representations of a con man."

Two doctors have admitted knowingly buying the foreign drugs. One of them, a Pennsylvania oncologist whose practice purchased nearly $1 million worth of the misbranded drugs, was recently fined $100,000 and ordered to place ads in two medical journals warning of the dangers of unapproved drugs.

Between 2005 and 2011, Bean illegally sold more than $7 million worth of prescription oncology drugs to doctors in the U.S. Cancer medicine is expensive, Godshall explained. "A single course of chemotherapy can cost hundreds of thousands of dollars." At the same time, many cancer patients being treated by oncologists are eligible for Medicare, and reimbursements to doctors from Medicare have been cut, providing further incentive for physicians to buy non-approved discounted drugs. "All those factors added to Bean being able to successfully carry on his fraud for so long," Godshall said.

The drugs Bean fraudulently sold turned out to be the foreign equivalents of the same drugs manufactured for the U.S. market. But without FDA oversight, there is no guarantee that drugs coming into the country illegally aren't counterfeit and unsafe, Godshall said. "The point of the law is to protect our supply chain here in the United States and to protect the health of American citizens."

He added, "You go to a doctor and expect that they are going to treat your disease and not knowingly expose you to any dangers. But when doctors use drugs that have not been approved by the FDA, there's no telling what you are getting. And that puts a patient's health in jeopardy."

Serial Killers
Part 2: The Birth of Behavioral Analysis in the FBI

In the final days of 1977, a man now known as one of the most prolific serial killers in U.S. history—Theodore "Ted" Bundy—cleverly escaped from a Colorado prison while most of the staff was away for the holidays.

FBI agents quickly joined the search. In early February 1978, the Bureau placed Bundy on its Ten Most Wanted Fugitives list. Among the information shared by the FBI with law enforcement during this time were details on his "M.O." (modus operandi or method of operation). Bundy typically looked for victims at places where young people gathered, such as colleges, beaches, ski resorts, and discos, the FBI explained. And he preferred young, attractive women with long hair parted in the middle.

The synopsis was pulled from a psychological assessment of Ted Bundy prepared by two FBI agents—Howard Teten and Robert Ressler—at the Bureau's Training Academy. The two men were part of a groundbreaking behavioral analysis unit set up five years earlier for precisely this purpose: to study the behavior, experiences, and psychological make-up of criminals and suspects for patterns and insights that could help solve cases and prevent future crimes, especial serial murders and other forms of violence.

Criminal behavioral analysis wasn't a new concept. In the 1940s and 1950s, for example, George Metsky—the so-called "Mad Bomber"—planted explosive devices around New York City until a behavioral profile developed for the police by a local criminologist and psychiatrist helped lead to his capture in 1957. But in the coming years, the FBI would take this innovation to a whole new level.

At the center of this evolution was Teten. He had joined the FBI as an agent in 1962, already with an interest in the psychological aspects of criminal behavior. In 1969, he was recruited by the Training Division to be an instructor, and around 1970, he convinced his supervisor to let him teach a workshop in "applied criminology." His first course was a four-hour lecture to New York police; it was a hit. Next, he gave the course at a regional police training school in Texas, expanding it to four days. By about day three, students were bringing up unsolved cases. Based on insights from a class discussion, one student interviewed a suspect—and the man confessed.

Behavioral analysis played a role in the case of serial killer Ted Bundy.

Word spread, and interest in the course skyrocketed. So Teten borrowed FBI New York Special Agent Patrick Mullany, who had a master's degree in educational psychology, and the two began teaching together. Teten would outline the facts of a case, and Mullany would show how aspects of the criminal's personality were revealed in the crime scene. According to Teten, "Patrick really made a difference, because he was a fully qualified psychologist, where I was a criminologist." Soon Mullany was reassigned to Quantico permanently.

In 1972, the FBI stood up a behavioral science unit to advance the concepts the pair was teaching throughout the FBI and across law enforcement; it was led by Supervisory Special Agent Jack Kirsch and included Teten and Mullany (Ressler joined in 1975)—and their growing education, research, and service responsibilities. As the unit developed, so did the FBI's study and understanding of serial killers.

And Ted Bundy? Five days after landing on the FBI's Top Ten list, he was caught by a Florida policeman. He was ultimately convicted of multiple murders and executed in 1989.

Part 3: Ted Bundy's campaign of terror (page 83)

Left: Hovhannes Harutyunyan, center, an Armenian who was living in Burbank, California, is one of the architects of a fraud ring that enlisted visa holders like Yermek Dossymbekov, left, and Alisher Omarov to commit crimes. If you have information on the case, contact the San Diego FBI at (858) 320-1800 or submit a tip at tips.fbi.gov.

International Fraud
Crime Ring Recruited Short-Term Visa Holders

The recruitment pitch to students on short-term visas must have seemed irresistible: give us your good name and some help in our fraud scheme, and we'll put money—potentially thousands of dollars—in your wallet before your return trip home.

In charges unsealed late last month in San Diego, FBI agents and their law enforcement partners named dozens of young visa holders from former Soviet bloc countries who took the bait and became willing co-conspirators in a range of elaborate fraud schemes. In four separate indictments, a federal grand jury laid bare how a Los Angeles-based Armenian crime ring ran scams in L.A. and San Diego that relied on a steady tide of accomplices whose time was short in the U.S. While the crimes themselves were not especially novel—identity theft, bank fraud, tax fraud—the explicit recruitment of co-conspirators with expiring visas was a twist.

"The J-1 visa holders are a commodity in these cases," said Special Agent Davene Butler, who works in our San Diego Division. She described how a few masterminds enlisted young accomplices to do much of the legwork in their fraud schemes—opening bank accounts and securing apartments and post office boxes to route proceeds from bogus tax returns, for example. By the time a scam came to light, the "foot soldiers" holding J-1 and F-1 visas—which allow foreigners to study and travel in the U.S. for brief periods—would be long gone. "They were essential in the schemes," Butler said.

The charges announced on September 26 named 55 individuals and followed a two-year investigation led by the San Diego FBI, local authorities, and the IRS, which paid out more than $7 million in bogus tax refunds. About half of those charged were arrested last month in a nationwide sweep, but more than 25 remain at large, including 24 who are believed to have left the country. The FBI is asking for the public's help locating some of the suspects, including one of the crime ring's main architects, Hovhannes Harutyunyan, 34, an Armenian whose last known address was in Burbank, California.

The charges show four primary schemes. Here's how they worked:

- Using stolen identities, the crime ring filed about 2,000 fraudulent tax returns claiming more than $20 million in refunds. J-1 students obtained addresses and bank accounts for the fraudulent refunds to be sent.

- Conspirators set up bank accounts and began writing checks back and forth to create a good transaction history, which banks rewarded by shortening or eliminating holds on deposited checks. Then the so-called "seed" accounts wrote bad checks to 60 "bust-out" accounts, which paid out more than $680,000.

- Conspirators obtained personal information about the identities and accounts of wealthy bank customers and disguised themselves as the account holders. They practiced forging documents and impersonating the account holders and succeeded in obtaining $551,842. They laundered the money by purchasing gold with the stolen funds.

- Conspirators obtained pre-paid debit cards in the names of identity theft victims and opened bank accounts in the names of visa holders who sold their account information before leaving the U.S. They then filed more than 400 fraudulent tax returns seeking more than $3 million.

"This investigation involved multiple complex fraudulent schemes resulting in significant losses to financial institutions and American taxpayers," said San Diego FBI Special Agent in Charge Daphne Hearn.

Agent Butler said the charges and arrests send a message that these schemes are not without consequences. Those who have already fled won't find it easy to get back to the U.S. "And they won't be able to tell their friends that they can come to the U.S., commit fraud, get some quick cash, and that nothing will happen to them," she said.

Note: The fugitives pictured here may have been located since the above information was posted on our website. Please check www.fbi.gov for up-to-date information.

The Risks to the Thin Blue Line

Latest *Law Enforcement Officers Killed and Assaulted* Report Released

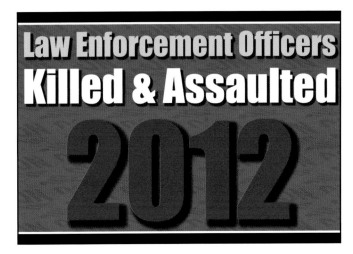

A Florida detective was shot and killed while investigating a residence believed to house a meth lab. An Arizona deputy sheriff lost his life responding to a burglary alarm at a business. A Washington state park ranger was shot and killed after she attempted to conduct a traffic stop.

These three law enforcement officers were among the 48 officers around the nation who died in 2012 as a result of felonious incidents in the line of duty, according to the FBI's latest *Law Enforcement Officers Killed and Assaulted* (LEOKA) report. All 48 officers would have undoubtedly considered their actions a part of the job. But the duties performed by these brave men and women—and others just like them—are far from routine, and this latest report continues to highlight the risks law enforcement officers face on a daily basis.

Among the report's findings:

- The average age of the officers feloniously killed in action in 2012 was 38; they had an average of 12 years of service.

- The victims worked in a variety of positions—many on vehicle patrol but also as detectives, officers on special assignments, undercover officers, etc.

- They died in a variety of situations—arrests, traffic pursuits or stops, investigations of suspicious persons or circumstances, ambushes, tactical situations, disturbance calls, and more.

- Six of the slain officers were off-duty but felt duty-bound to intercede and were acting in an official capacity at the time of the incidents.

- Of the 48 officers killed, 44 were killed with firearms.

Our latest LEOKA report also provides information on another 47 officers who died during 2012 as a result of accidents sustained in the line of duty and on the 52,901 law enforcement officers assaulted in the line of duty.

LEOKA's overall goal is to reduce law enforcement deaths and assaults. By providing agencies with detailed descriptions of circumstances leading to officer fatalities and injuries every year, police training programs can be continuously enhanced to help officers stay safe during similar situations.

Beyond publishing the LEOKA report, the FBI has other initiatives that are designed to help protect law enforcement. For example:

- Our LEOKA program also offers an officer safety awareness training course that provides potentially life-saving information to help law enforcement personnel improve their situational awareness during activities like arrests, traffic stops, foot pursuits, ambushes, and other high-risk encounters.

- The FBI Academy's one-week Law Enforcement Training for Safety and Survival program is designed to give participants the skills and mindset required to identify and handle critical situations in high-risk environments. Topics include arrest planning, ballistic shield deployment, low light operations, felony vehicle stops, and basic survival techniques.

- Our National Crime Information Center (NCIC)—accessed by more than 92,000 agencies—added a Violent Persons File in 2012 that can help officers quickly determine if, during a routine traffic stop or another type of encounter, they come across an individual who has a violent criminal history or who has previously threatened law enforcement.

Law enforcement will always be a dangerous profession, but enhanced training and awareness will better protect those who join its ranks.

Attorney-Turned-Racketeer
'Stunning' Betrayal of the Law

Earlier this year, a man was put on trial in a federal courtroom in Newark, New Jersey. From the list of charges—nearly two dozen in all—he sounded like a gang leader, drug lord, or organized crime boss. He was accused of running a criminal enterprise, conspiring to murder a federal witness, committing wire fraud, distributing cocaine, and facilitating prostitution, bribery, and other crimes.

But the individual who was ultimately convicted on 23 criminal counts and sentenced to life in prison was actually a high-powered Newark lawyer, a former New Jersey state and federal prosecutor-turned defense attorney.

His name is Paul Bergrin, and, in the end, he sacrificed the oath he had once taken to protect and defend the Constitution of the United States for the chance to line his own pockets. As New Jersey U.S. Attorney Paul J. Fishman said following the jury conviction, "Bergrin's conduct was a stunning violation of his role as an officer of the court and a betrayal of his roots as a member of law enforcement."

For years, Bergrin and his law firm were highly successful. His busy client roster ran the gamut—from famous celebrities to gang leaders and drug traffickers. He was a man-about-town who wore expensive suits, drove luxury cars, and rarely lost a case.

But after the 2004 murder of a federal informant who had damaging information about one of Bergrin's criminal clients, the FBI began an investigation. We uncovered evidence that revealed Bergrin was using his law offices as a cover to conduct illegal activities to protect his criminal clients from prosecution and carry on their unlawful pursuits. He used his position as a criminal defense attorney to manipulate and disrupt court proceedings on behalf of his clients.

And of course, he was paid handsomely for all of it.

Among Bergrin's criminal actions:

- Counseling, intimidating, and sometimes bribing witnesses to offer perjured testimony in favor of his clients or to flee so they wouldn't be available to testify;

- Coaching an 8-year-old murder witness to lie on the stand, resulting in the acquittal of one of his clients;

- Conspiring with clients to identify, locate, and murder witnesses who would testify against them;

- Using his law firm to launder money for clients, associates, and himself and to set up phony corporations or other legal entities to facilitate even more crimes;

- Running a drug trafficking operation and a prostitution business for two of his clients while they were in jail.

Bergrin had so many crimes on his plate that he recruited others—including his girlfriend (who worked at the law firm), his law partner, and one of his criminal clients—to take part in his racketeering enterprise. All told, eight of the nine individuals charged in the 2009 indictment pled guilty.

The probe into Bergrin and his co-conspirators was complex and involved investigators from the FBI, the Internal Revenue Service-Criminal Investigations, and the Drug Enforcement Administration. After a 2011 trial which ended with a hung jury, his 2013 trial (Bergrin represented himself at both trials) ended a bit differently—the jury quickly found him guilty on all counts.

The case was proof once again that those entrusted with the guardianship of our legal system are not above the law.

Fugitives Sought
New Subjects Added to Cyber's Most Wanted List

Five individuals have been added to our Cyber's Most Wanted list for their roles in domestic and international hacking and fraud crimes collectively involving hundreds of thousands of victims and tens of millions of dollars in losses.

In announcing the addition of the new subjects—along with rewards of up to $100,000 for information leading to their arrests—Executive Assistant Director of our Criminal, Cyber, Response, and Services Branch Richard McFeely said, "Throughout its history, the FBI has depended on the public's help and support to bring criminals to justice. That was true in the gangster era, and it's just as true in the cyber era. We need the public's help to catch these individuals who have made it their mission to spy on and steal from our nation and our citizens."

The new fugitives on our Cyber's Most Wanted list are:

- Pakistani nationals Farhan Arshad and Noor Aziz Uddin, wanted for their alleged involvement in an international telecommunications hacking scheme. Between 2008 and 2012, the pair gained unauthorized access to business telephone systems, resulting in losses exceeding $50 million. Arshad and Uddin are part of an international criminal ring that the FBI believes extends into Pakistan, the Philippines, Saudi Arabia, Switzerland, Spain, Singapore, Italy, Malaysia and elsewhere.

- Carlos Perez-Melara, wanted for a variety of cyber crimes—including running a fraudulent website in 2003 that offered customers a way to "catch a cheating lover." Those who took the bait downloaded spyware that secretly installed a program on their computers that allowed scammers to steal the victims' identities and personal information.

- Syrian national Andrey Nabilevich Taame, wanted for his alleged role in Operation Ghost Click, a malware scheme that compromised more than four million computers in more than 100 countries between 2007 and October 2011; there were at least 500,000 victims in the United States alone.

- Russian national Alexsey Belan, wanted for allegedly remotely accessing the computer networks of three U.S.-based companies in 2012 and 2013 and stealing sensitive data as well as employees' identities.

Rewards are being offered for each of the five fugitives, all of whom are believed to be living outside the U.S.

The FBI's Most Wanted program is best known for its Ten Most Wanted Fugitives list. The Top Ten list was established more than six decades ago and has become a symbol of the Bureau's crime-fighting ability around the world. But the Bureau highlights other wanted fugitives as well—terrorists, white-collar criminals, and increasingly, those who commit cyber crimes.

The FBI leads the national effort to investigate high-tech crimes, including cyber-based terrorism, espionage, computer intrusions, and major cyber fraud. The expansion of the Cyber's Most Wanted list is a reflection of the FBI's increased efforts in this area, McFeely said. "The cyber fugitives we seek have caused significant losses to individuals and to our economy," he explained. "And cyber crime continues to pose a significant threat to our national security."

We need your help. If you have information about any of the five individuals mentioned above or the other fugitives on our Cyber's Most Wanted list, please submit a tip on our website or contact your local FBI office or the nearest U.S. Embassy or Consulate.

Note: The fugitives pictured here may have been located since the above information was posted on our website. Please check our Cyber's Most Wanted webpage at www.fbi.gov/wanted/cyber for up-to-date information.

Public Corruption
Inside the Kwame Kilpatrick Case

When Kwame Kilpatrick became mayor of Detroit in 2002, he promised to revitalize the city. Instead, he shamelessly used his position to steal from the citizens he had vowed to serve.

"Criminal activity was a way of life for him, and he constantly used the power of his office to look for new opportunities to make money illegally," said Special Agent Robert Beeckman, who investigated the mayor and his corrupt regime for eight years.

Last month, a federal judge sentenced Kilpatrick to a 28-year prison term for his role in a wide-ranging racketeering conspiracy that included extortion, bribery, and fraud. Thirty-two others have also been convicted of crimes in connection with the case, including Kilpatrick's contractor friend Bobby Ferguson, who received a 21-year jail term.

Kilpatrick and Ferguson established a "pay to play" system that made breaking the law standard operating procedure. Kilpatrick extorted city vendors, rigged bids, and took bribes. He used funds from non-profit civic organizations to line his pockets and those of his family. And he was unabashed about it.

"His crimes were not the result of a momentary lapse in judgment," said a document prepared for the court by the U.S. Attorney's Office for the Eastern District of Michigan. "He systematically exploited his office to enrich himself, his friends, and his family." For example, Kilpatrick and Ferguson obtained more than $500,000 from the state of Michigan and private donors for non-profit organizations they controlled. The organizations were supposed to help the community. Instead, the mayor spent large sums on himself for luxury vacations, spa treatments, and golf clubs.

The FBI opened a case on Kilpatrick in 2004, two years after he moved into the mayor's mansion. "Initially, we had sources and a few cooperating defendants from other cases who revealed a pay to play scheme and that the mayor was behind it," Beeckman said.

As the investigation unfolded, our agents—along with investigators from the Internal Revenue Service and other agencies—used court-ordered wiretaps and undercover operators to gather evidence. "Over the years, we employed every investigative technique we could," Beeckman said.

A significant break in the case came when investigators discovered that Kilpatrick's cell phone provider had kept an archive of all his text messages. "The messages were explicit," Beeckman said. "He talked about bid rigging, bribes, and other criminal activity. He had no idea there would be a record of those messages."

Investigators also followed the money, which left no doubt about Kilpatrick's corruption. Before he became mayor, Kilpatrick's paycheck from the state of Michigan was electronically deposited into his bank account, and he made regular withdrawals to pay bills and to get cash. After his election, he stopped making withdrawals and instead made only large cash deposits.

Kilpatrick's bank records revealed more than $840,000 in unexplained expenditures above and beyond his salary as mayor—and none of that money was disclosed on his tax returns. "There were times," Beeckman said, "when the mayor would hand one of the officers on his protective detail an envelope with cash and tell him to take it to the bank and pay his credit card bill."

The beleaguered mayor pled guilty to two felony counts in 2008 and resigned his office. Two years later, he was indicted for mail fraud, wire fraud, and tax evasion; in March 2013 he was found guilty of the wide-ranging racketeering conspiracy charges.

Why was Kilpatrick so brazen about his crimes? "He thought he was above the law," Beeckman believes. "He thought he could do whatever he wanted and get away with it."

That turned out not to be the case, thanks to the dedicated work of the investigators and prosecutors who brought Kilpatrick and his co-conspirators to justice.

Serial Killers
Part 3: Ted Bundy's Campaign of Terror

No one knows when or where Theodore "Ted" Bundy killed for the first time. It could have been during his teenage years or when he was in his early 20s in the late 1960s. It might have been in Washington state, where he resided for many years, or on the East Coast, where he was born and lived as a young boy and had family ties.

But we do know that by 1974, Ted Bundy's prolific reign of terror and murder was underway. In Washington state, young, attractive female college students began disappearing. Local police investigated, and clues began to emerge. Witnesses pointed to a Volkswagen Beetle and a young man on crutches or with an arm in a sling.

Bundy moved to Salt Lake City that summer, and the murders continued in Utah, Idaho, and Colorado. In August 1975, police arrested Bundy for the first time after pulling him over in his Volkswagen and finding suspicious items—including handcuffs, rope, and a ski mask—that investigators later linked to missing women. In February of the following year, he was found guilty of kidnapping and assaulting a Utah teenager who had managed to escape from him, landing in prison for up to 15 years.

Meanwhile, investigators from multiple states were piecing together the string of murders. In 1976, Bundy was charged with killing a vacationing nursing student, and he found himself in Aspen, Colorado in June 1977 for a preliminary hearing. Left alone at one point, Bundy let himself out of a second story window, jogged down Main Street, and disappeared. Extensive searches were made, and the FBI quickly began to gather and disseminate Bundy's criminal history and identification information. Soon after, FBI agents swore out a federal arrest warrant for unlawful flight to avoid confinement, and a $100,000 reward was offered for his capture.

Bundy didn't make it far; he was located in Aspen a few days later. But he bided his time and seized another opportunity for escape on New Year's Eve in 1977—slipping through an opening in the ceiling of his cell and sneaking out through the jailer's office.

A nationwide manhunt followed, and the FBI played a central role. We created a series of wanted posters and other identification material, processed latent fingerprints

A $100,000 reward was offered for Ted Bundy's capture.

from around the country, provided insight from our Behavioral Analysis Unit, and—as the days stretched into weeks—added Bundy to our Ten Most Wanted Fugitives list on February 10, 1977.

Tragically, Bundy continued his murder spree while on the run. On the evening of January 14, he invaded a Florida State University sorority house, brutally killing two co-eds and leaving a third with serious injuries.

But the net was closing. Around 1:30 a.m. on February 15, a Pensacola police officer noticed a stolen orange Volkswagen Beetle driving west on Cervantes Street and ordered the car to pull over. Bundy resisted but was eventually taken into custody.

The officer had no idea who was inside the car, but Bundy was quickly identified with the help of the FBI's fugitive flyer and was soon back in Colorado to face murder charges. He was eventually convicted and executed, but not before admitting to more than two dozen murders over many years. There may have been even more. To this day, Ted Bundy remains one of the nation's most deadly and notorious serial killers.

Note: This series will continue in 2014.

Taking Stock
Corporate Execs Get Scammed

It was a slick financial scam. A company that claimed to be an institutional lender offered loans to corporate executives, accepted as collateral the stock that the executives held in their publicly traded companies, and then—unbeknownst to those executives—sold their stock out from under them.

But at its core, it was also a classic Ponzi scheme, a nearly century-old criminal technique that involves using proceeds stolen from victims as a way to keep a fraud going as long as possible.

After an investigation by FBI San Diego—with assistance from the Securities and Exchange Commission—the president of the company, Douglas McClain, Jr., was tried and convicted this past May in connection with this securities fraud scheme. (Included in the 2012 indictment was McClain's partner, James Miceli, who died shortly before trial.) Just recently, McClain was sentenced to 15 years in federal prison and ordered to pay $81 million in restitution to his victims and to forfeit millions in ill-gotten gains, including cash and securities, a luxury home and car, a houseboat, and diamond jewelry.

McClain ran Argyll Equities, Inc., a company that operated in several U.S. states, including California. From at least 2004 to 2011, the company advertised itself as an institutional lender with significant assets that made loans to corporate officers and directors who may have been going through some professional hard times, wanted to expand their operations, or needed cash for personal reasons. And even though most were paper-rich because of their stock holdings, as company "insiders" they were not permitted to sell their stocks outright because of federal securities laws and regulations.

McClain conspired with loan brokers to fraudulently induce corporate executives—from the U.S. and abroad—to pledge millions of dollars of stock as collateral in return for a loan. These loans were attractive to corporate executives: by using their stock as collateral, they would receive a loan for typically 30 to 50 percent less than the current market value of their shares, and, unless they missed a loan payment or saw a significant drop in stock prices, they would get their stock back upon repayment.

In reality, though, Argyll had no intention of giving the stocks back. They were quickly sold on the open market, sometimes even before the loans closed. And since Argyll had no other source of income, proceeds from the sale of the stocks were what McClain used to fund the loans…and he pocketed the difference between the loan amount and what the stocks actually sold for.

At the end of the loan term, the borrowers expected to get their stocks back, but McClain was full of phony excuses as to why that wasn't happening—the stocks were tied up in a hedge fund, the borrower had defaulted on the loan by missing a payment, etc. And in some cases, selling the stocks caused a drop in stock prices, which in turn caused an actual loan default.

The moral of the story? Whether you're a high-powered company executive or getting paid by the hour, before entering into a business arrangement, do your due diligence—research the individuals/companies involved, consult an independent third-party expert, and above all, remember that if sounds too good to be true, it probably is.

The JFK Assassination
Former Agent Recalls His Role in the Investigation

On that autumn Friday 50 years ago today, when John F. Kennedy's motorcade was turning onto Dealey Plaza in Dallas just beneath the Texas School Book Depository, Robert Frazier was at work at FBI Headquarters in Washington. The 44-year-old special agent—the Bureau's lead firearms and ballistics examiner—had no idea that he was about to be given the most important assignment of his career.

Former Special Agent Robert Frazier, 94, talks about working on the Kennedy assassination investigation.

"It was around 11:30 that morning when we first heard about the shooting," Frazier said recently at his Northern Virginia home. Now 94, memories of events that transpired five decades ago are indelibly etched in his mind.

After learning of the assassination, the chief of the FBI Laboratory called in Frazier and two other veteran examiners. Frazier recalls the chief's instructions: "He said, 'I want each of you men to make separate comparisons and examinations, and then compare your notes and see if they agree.'"

By that evening, as a shocked country tried to comprehend Kennedy's assassination, FBI agents and other federal officers had already begun delivering evidence to the FBI Laboratory—then located in Washington—including the rifle that Lee Harvey Oswald used to kill the president.

Well after midnight, Frazier and his colleagues went to the Secret Service garage to gather evidence from the presidential limousine. The vehicle had been flown from Dallas back to Washington that afternoon. "We examined that car very thoroughly that same night," Frazier said.

That was the first of many sleepless nights for Frazier and his fellow examiners as the investigation unfolded. "We never got home Friday night or Saturday, but we got home Sunday for about five hours of sleep," he recalled. Frazier's wife wanted to attend Kennedy's funeral procession along Pennsylvania Avenue that Monday, he said, and he accompanied her. "Then I went back to work and didn't get home again until Wednesday."

Over the course of the next two years, Frazier immersed himself in the investigation. He traveled to Dallas and positioned himself at the same sixth-floor book depository window where Oswald waited for the presidential motorcade to come into view. "We re-enacted the entire thing very, very carefully," he said. "I stood up there and we took Oswald's rifle, with the scope on it, and set it up." He also examined the revolver Oswald used to kill Dallas Police Officer J.D. Tippit shortly before he was apprehended.

Frazier, who testified several times before the Warren Commission regarding his findings, is well aware of the many conspiracy theories surrounding the Kennedy assassination—but he remains convinced that Oswald was the only shooter. "There has never been anything to indicate positively that anybody else was involved," he said.

Beyond the facts of the case and the volumes of findings Frazier's firearms and ballistic examinations produced, the assassination still evokes an emotional response from him 50 years later. "It was a sad situation," he said. "Just remembering that it was Kennedy and what a personality he had. … It was a terrible, terrible thing."

Frazier is proud of the work he did on what turned out to be the most significant case of his career. All these years later, he is confident that the work he and his colleagues conducted was meticulous and thorough. "We knew we did the best that could have been done."

Scan this QR code with your smartphone to access a related video, or visit www.fbi.gov/jfk50years.

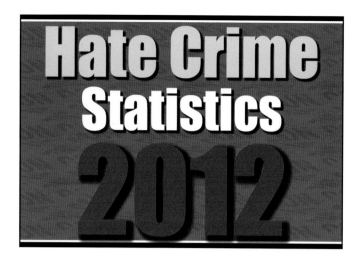

Latest Hate Crime Statistics
Annual Report Shows Slight Decrease

The FBI has just released its hate crime statistics report for 2012, and the numbers show that we as a nation still have a way to go toward alleviating these crimes that have such a devastating impact on communities.

For the 2012 time frame, law enforcement agencies reported 5,796 hate crime incidents involving 6,718 offenses, down from 2011 figures of 6,222 incidents involving 7,254 offenses. Also during 2012, there were 7,164 hate crime victims reported (which include individuals, businesses, institutions, and society as a whole), down from 7,713 in 2011.

The data contained in *Hate Crime Statistics, 2012* is a subset of the information that law enforcement submits to the FBI's Uniform Crime Reporting (UCR) Program. The full hate crime report can be viewed on our website, but here are a few highlights:

- 48.3 percent of the 5,790 single-bias incidents were racially motivated, while 19.6 percent resulted from sexual orientation bias and 19 percent from religious bias.

- Of the 7,164 hate crime victims, 55.4 percent were victims of crimes against persons and 41.8 percent were victims of crimes against property. The remaining 2.8 percent were victims of crimes against society (like drug offenses, gambling, and prostitution).

- 39.6 percent of the victims of crimes against persons suffered simple assaults, while 37.5 percent were intimidated and 21.5 percent were victims of aggravated assault. (Law enforcement also reported 10 murders and 15 rapes as hate crimes.)

- An overwhelming majority—75.6 percent—of the victims of crimes against property were victimized by acts of destruction, damage, and/or vandalism.

- Of the 5,331 known offenders, 54.6 percent were white and 23.3 percent were black.

Recent Changes to Hate Crime Data Collection

Beginning in January of this year, new UCR data collection methods were enacted, allowing law enforcement to get even more specific when submitting bias motivation information. For example, as a result of the Matthew Shepard and James Byrd, Jr. Hate Crime Prevention Act, agencies can now report on crimes motivated by "gender identity" bias and "crimes committed by, and crimes directed against, juveniles." And a federal directive enabled our UCR Program to expand and/or modify its data collection categories for race and ethnicity. (This enhanced 2013 hate crime data will be published in 2014.)

FBI's Role in Combating Hate Crimes

In addition to our annual hate crime report—published to help provide a more accurate accounting of the problem—the FBI is the sole investigative force for criminal violations of federal civil rights statutes. As a matter of fact, hate crime is the number one priority in our civil rights program, and we opened some 200 hate crime investigations during 2012.

But in addition to our investigations, we also work closely with our state and local partners on their investigations—offering FBI resources, forensic expertise, and experience in identifying and proving hate-based motivations. We participate in hate crime working groups around the country to help develop strategies that address local problems. And we conduct training for local law enforcement, minority and religious organizations, and community groups to reduce civil rights abuses.

NICS Turns 15
Stats Show Success of FBI's Gun Background Check System

Fifteen years ago, on November 30, 1998, the FBI flipped the switch on the National Instant Criminal Background Check System, or NICS, a provision of the 1993 Brady Act that requires background checks on individuals purchasing firearms or receiving them through some other means.

The goal at the time was to disqualify any transfers of firearms to ineligible individuals while at the same time ensuring timely transactions for eligible individuals. Today, as the FBI-run background check system marks its anniversary, successes are seen daily and in real-time on both fronts.

Since its inception, the NICS has processed more than 177 million background checks requested by gun sellers, or federal firearms licensees (FFLs). On its busiest days, the system processes more than 10,000 automated checks an hour across 94 million records in FBI criminal databases, including the National Crime Information Center (NCIC), the Interstate Identification Index (III), and the NICS index of 11 million individuals who fall into certain categories that prohibit them from receiving firearms. Nine out of 10 NICS determinations are instantaneous, so FFLs know immediately whether to proceed with transactions or deny them. To date, NICS queries of criminal databases have resulted in 1,065,090 denials, with 88,479 in 2012 alone.

"The statistics for denials can stand on their own with regards to how well the system works in keeping firearms out of the hands of those who shouldn't have them," said Steve Fischer, a spokesman for the NICS, which is run by the Bureau's Criminal Justice Information Services (CJIS) Division in West Virginia.

The most common reasons for denials are prior criminal convictions, domestic violence, drug history, and fugitive status.

In 37 states, NICS background checks are conducted by the FBI when purchases are initiated at one of the country's 46,895 licensed gun sellers. The sellers contact the NICS through an online electronic system or through one of three call centers, which run the names against the databases. Thirteen states perform their own background checks by utilizing the NICS.

A NICS examiner reviews background information to determine if prohibitive criteria exists.

While most NICS checks return immediate dispositions of "proceed" or "deny," about eight percent are delayed, usually because of incomplete criminal history records. By law, the NICS section must make a determination within three days or the transaction may be allowed to proceed. It's during that period that NICS staff research missing information to update the records and create a clearer picture of applicants. Last year alone, the NICS section filled in the blanks on more than 34,000 incomplete criminal history records and then shared the information with state agencies.

Records are not kept on individuals whose transactions are approved to proceed. By law, they are purged within 24 hours. NICS has an appeal process in place for individuals whose transactions are denied.

In addition to firearms, the Safe Explosives Act of 2003 requires background checks as part of the licensing process for individuals shipping or receiving explosives. The requests are submitted to NICS by the Bureau of Alcohol, Tobacco, Firearms, and Explosives (ATF), and the ATF makes the final determinations. To date, the NICS has processed more than 700,000 explosives background checks; in 2012, the NICS processed 148,856 checks and denied 3,077.

The NICS employs nearly 500 people and operates 17 hours a day (8 a.m. to 1 a.m.), 364 days a year (closed on Christmas). The system can—and does—routinely process more than 80,000 requests a day. Last December, the NICS processed 2.7 million background checks—177,170 in a single day on December 21. According to a 2012 NICS report, the highest volume of background check requests usually occurs on the day after Thanksgiving.

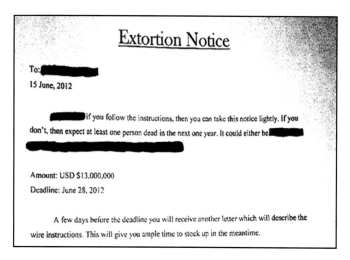

Extortion Notice

To: ███████

15 June, 2012

███████ if you follow the instructions, then you can take this notice lightly. If you don't, then expect at least one person dead in the next one year. It could either be ███████
███████████████████████████

Amount: USD $13,000,000
Deadline: June 28, 2012

A few days before the deadline you will receive another letter which will describe the wire instructions. This will give you ample time to stock up in the meantime.

Left: An excerpt of a letter from Vivek Shah, who attempted to extort more than $120 million from seven prominent victims.

Attempted Extortion
Aspiring Actor's New Role: Inmate

It was an outrageous plan worthy of a Hollywood thriller. But an aspiring actor's real-life attempt to extort tens of millions of dollars from wealthy targets earned him decidedly bad reviews in federal court and a new role for the next seven years—as a prison inmate.

Vivek Shah was pursuing an acting career in Los Angeles in 2012 when he thought of a better way to make money than from the bit parts he had landed in movies. He planned to extort billionaires—a coal tycoon and movie producer among them—by threatening to kill members of their families if they didn't pay.

"He was very ambitious," said Special Agent Jim Lafferty, who works out of our Pittsburgh Division and specializes in white-collar crime. Shah, 26, attempted to extort more than $120 million from seven prominent victims, including movie producer Harvey Weinstein ($4 million demanded), Groupon co-founder Eric Lefkofsky ($16 million demanded), coal executive Chris Cline ($13 million demanded), and oil and gas billionaire Terry Pegula ($34 million demanded).

He chose victims after doing online research about the world's wealthiest people, and his targets were instructed to wire money to offshore bank accounts. To set up those accounts, Shah needed a proof of address, so he established a Post Office Box in Los Angeles using a fake driver's license bearing the name Ray Amin.

"He had the fake ID created for the sole purpose of opening the PO Box," Lafferty said. "He purchased it from someone who makes false IDs for underage college students." Shah used various other means to avoid detection—like conducting online research from public places that provided anonymous Wi-Fi and using prepaid debit cards to purchase postage online for the extortion letters.

But things didn't turn out as he planned. Shah had been involved in a domestic dispute with his roommate several weeks before he established the PO Box. When police were called to the scene in May 2012, they discovered the fake ID, which they checked against the FBI's National Crime Information Center (NCIC) database. Shah told the officers he was an actor and that the bogus driver's license was merely a prop. The NCIC check confirmed that no criminal activity was associated with the name Ray Amin.

Later, when agents discovered that "Ray Amin" had opened the PO Box connected with the extortion scheme, they ran their own NCIC check, and Shah's name came back associated with Amin.

From there, agents were able to monitor Shah's real online accounts, which led from California to Chicago, where video surveillance showed him mailing more extortion letters. The FBI Laboratory later matched his DNA with the letters. Shah was arrested in August 2012, pled guilty to the extortion scheme in May 2013, and was sentenced in September. Lafferty credits the U.S. Attorney's Office for the Southern District of West Virginia with helping to bring the investigation to a quick and successful resolution.

After his arrest, Shah claimed his plan was to draw attention to himself. "He imagined the case going public and him gaining notoriety and somehow benefitting from that," Lafferty said. "That obviously didn't happen."

Although the fake ID quickly led agents to Shah, Lafferty noted that the crime was ill-advised from the start. "The technology and investigative capability the FBI and our partners possess would make it extremely difficult to pull off an extortion scheme like this," he said. "He really never had a chance."

Billion-Dollar Investment Fraud
Undercover Agents Uncover the Scheme

For a group of financial fraudsters, it seemed like the ultimate get in an investment scam—a victim willing to hand over $1 billion.

However, like victims of financial scams everywhere, these criminals should have paid more attention to the "if it sounds too good to be true, it probably is" adage—the wealthy "victim" in this case was actually an undercover FBI agent. And last month, the last three members of this group of con artists were sentenced to federal prison for their role in this scam. Several co-conspirators have previously pled guilty.

Beginning in 2005, the two-year undercover operation named Collateral Monte took leads from previous complaints, victim referrals, cooperating witnesses, and information from regulatory agencies and specifically targeted criminals who lured potential victims with offers of substantial returns on investments with little or no risk (also known as high-yield investment programs). And because the Orange County, California area served as an ideal backdrop for wealthy victim-investors, it was there that we set up a bogus financial advisory company purportedly to invest money from wealthy residents, including doctors and retirees. Our "company," however, never interacted with actual investors…just suspected con men.

This particular case got underway with an Internet posting from an individual claiming he had access to a "private placement program" where the funds were guaranteed by the Federal Reserve Bank (the Fed), that a $10 million investment would return $100 million after 50 weeks, and that he also had access to other private placement programs with greater return rates but required higher minimum investments.

We e-mailed the author of the posting and said we had a potential investor interested in the offer. Over the next few months, the scam's operators appeared to be working directly out of the high-yield investment scam playbook—our investor was first introduced to some lower-level players whose job was to basically vet potential investors to ensure they actually had the money they claimed. Eventually, members of our undercover team were introduced to others higher up the chain with official-

sounding titles: Fed trade administrator, compliance officer, underwriter, banking expert, bank liaison, and trader.

The scheme, which offered international investment opportunities through the trading of bank securities, gradually progressed to its ultimate goal—to gain control of all or a portion of the victim's money.

And along the way, our undercover "investor" was told various lies by the scammers, including:

- Only a privileged few were invited to participate in these types of investment opportunities and there were only a few traders in the world authorized to offer them.

- The investment program was regulated by the Federal Reserve Bank, had to follow strict federal guidelines, and was overseen by a Fed trade administrator and Fed compliance officer.

- The investment's extraordinary rates of return were the result of conducting multiple trades in rapid succession.

- One of the primary reasons these trading programs existed was to generate funds for humanitarian purposes and that a portion of the investor's profits must be used towards that end.

By October 2008, we had enough evidence—e-mails, phone calls, in-person meetings, etc.—to get a criminal indictment against eight co-conspirators. And by going after these criminals proactively, we were able to stop them before they harmed actual victims.

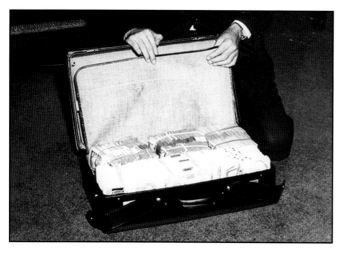

Left: Kidnappers demanded a ransom of $240,000 for Frank Sinatra, Jr. Agents used this suitcase for the cash provided by the Sinatra family.

A Byte Out of History
The Kidnapping of Frank Sinatra, Jr.

Five decades ago yesterday—just days after the assassination of President John F. Kennedy—a group of amateur criminals hoping to strike it rich engineered one of the most infamous kidnappings in American history.

For several weeks, two 23-year-old former high school classmates from Los Angeles—Barry Keenan and Joe Amsler—had been following a 19-year-old singer from city to city, waiting to make their move. Their target: none other than Frank Sinatra, Jr., son of one of the most famous singers in the world, "Old Blue Eyes" himself. Their plan was bold but simple…snatch the young Sinatra and demand a hefty ransom from his wealthy father.

The pair decided to strike on the evening of December 8, 1963. Sinatra, Jr., just beginning his career in music, was performing at Harrah's Club Lodge in Lake Tahoe on the border of California and Nevada. Around 9 p.m. he was resting in his dressing room with a friend when Keenan knocked on the door, pretending to be delivering a package. Keenan and Amsler entered, tied up Sinatra's friend with tape, and blindfolded their victim. They took him out a side door to their waiting car.

The singer's friend quickly freed himself and notified authorities. Roadblocks were set up, and the kidnappers were actually stopped by police…but they bluffed their way through and drove on to their hideout in a suburb of Los Angeles.

By 9:40, the FBI office in Reno was brought in on the case. Agents met with young Sinatra's father in Reno and his mother in Bel Air, California. The motive was presumed to be money. The FBI recommended that

Sinatra wait for a ransom demand, pay it, and then allow the Bureau to track the money and find the kidnappers.

The following evening, Keenan called a third conspirator, John Irwin, who was to be the ransom contact. Irwin called the elder Sinatra and told him to await the kidnappers' instructions. On December 10, he passed along the demand for $240,000 in ransom. Sinatra, Sr. gathered the money and gave it to the FBI, which photographed it all and made the drop per Keenan's instructions between two school buses in Sepulveda, California during the early morning hours of December 11.

While Keenan and Amsler picked up the money, Irwin had gotten nervous and decided to free the victim. Sinatra, Jr. was found in Bel Air after walking a few miles and alerting a security guard. To avoid the press, he was put in the trunk of the guard's patrol car and taken to his mother Nancy's home.

Young Sinatra described what he knew to FBI agents, but he had barely seen two of the kidnappers and only heard the voice of the third conspirator. Still, the Bureau tracked the clues back to the house where Sinatra had been held in Canoga Park and gathered even more evidence there.

Meanwhile, with the FBI's progress being recounted in the press, the criminals felt the noose tightening. Irwin broke first, spilling the beans to his brother, who called the FBI office in San Diego. Hours later, Keenan and Amsler were captured, and nearly all of the ransom was recovered.

Although the defense tried to argue that Frank Sinatra, Jr. had engineered the kidnapping as a publicity stunt, the FBI had strong evidence to the contrary. The clincher was a confession letter written earlier by Keenan and left in a safe-deposit box. In the end, Keenan, Amsler, and Irwin were all convicted.

TEDAC Marks 10-Year Anniversary
A Potent Weapon in the War on Terror

It has been 10 years since the FBI established the Terrorist Explosive Device Analytical Center (TEDAC), and since that time the multi-agency operation—sometimes referred to as America's bomb library—has become an essential tool in the nation's fight against terrorism.

Before TEDAC, no single government entity was responsible for analyzing and exploiting evidence and intelligence related to the improvised explosive devices (IEDs) used by international and domestic terrorists. Today, TEDAC coordinates all those efforts.

Located at the FBI Laboratory in Quantico, Virginia, "TEDAC is the government's single repository for IEDs," said Special Agent Greg Carl, TEDAC director. "The evidence and intelligence we gather from these explosives is used by law enforcement, the military, the intelligence community, and by our political decision-makers. There is no question that the work we have done—and continue to do—has helped to save American lives."

Whether bombs come from the battlefields of Afghanistan or from homegrown terrorists within our borders, TEDAC's 13 government agency partners and 17 external partners collect the devices and send them to TEDAC to be analyzed and catalogued.

"We exploit the devices forensically," said Carl, a veteran FBI agent who is also a bomb technician. The results are analyzed by TEDAC's Intelligence Unit and disseminated to law enforcement entities and the intelligence community to provide key intelligence on terrorist networks. "Based on the forensic evidence—DNA, fingerprints, and other biometrics—we try to identify the bomb maker and also make associations, linking devices together from separate incidents."

Since its creation in 2003, TEDAC has examined more than 100,000 IEDs from around the world and currently receives submissions at the rate of 800 per month. As a result, Carl said, "we have identified over 1,000 individuals with potential ties to terrorism."

Also based on TEDAC analysis, more than 100 people have been named to the government's Terrorist Watchlist, a database that identifies subjects known to

A TEDAC analyst catalogs evidence.

be or reasonably suspected of being involved in terrorist activity.

Subject matter experts from TEDAC can quickly deploy to incidents—such as the Boston Marathon bombings last April—and work with FBI Evidence Response Teams and local law enforcement to collect critical evidence and quickly transport it to the FBI Laboratory in Quantico for analysis.

TEDAC is capable of more than evidence collection for criminal prosecution, though. "Since we also partner with the military and the intelligence community, our work is utilized by many different sources," Carl said. The military, for example, uses TEDAC intelligence for force protection and to disrupt terror networks. Decision-makers can count on TEDAC's intelligence—based on forensic science—to help them form policy.

"And our interagency partners use TEDAC for research," Carl added, explaining that agencies can "check out" a bomb—much like a library book—for testing and further analysis. "We maintain all of the devices that we've collected going back to the inception of the center."

Looking back over a decade and forward to the future—TEDAC is building a state-of-the-art facility in Huntsville, Alabama—Carl said, "I see TEDAC as good government. The fact that you have multiple agencies coming together, working toward one common cause, without duplicating resources means that everyone benefits. And that helps make the country safer."

Scan this QR code with your smartphone to access related video and photos, or visit www.fbi.gov/tedacanniversary.

Legat Copenhagen
Partnerships Pay Dividends at Nordic Outpost

When militants attacked a gas processing facility in Algeria earlier this year, killing three Americans, the FBI already had a web of partners in place to help work the case. The network extended from Algiers, where the Bureau has an office, or legal attaché (legat), to the FBI's office in Copenhagen, Denmark, which maintains close ties with all the Nordic countries, to Norway, home to one of the gas facility's owners and five of the nearly 40 hostages killed there.

Throughout the siege, information flowed between agents on the ground, workers in hiding and their employers, Norwegian police, and the Bureau's International Operations Division, which runs 64 legat offices around the world. The familiar relationships—cultivated under less dire circumstances—helped authorities work to quickly assemble a picture of what was happening. The ensuing probe led to terrorism charges in July against a self-proclaimed al Qaeda leader in North Africa.

"We worked very closely with the Norwegian police to investigate the attack," said Special Agent Johannes Van Den Hoogen, the legal attaché in Copenhagen since 2012. "Throughout the crisis, we shared information about what we saw and heard. It's a great example of how we use our legat network to work with a partner in our area."

The case illustrates how relationships forged by our overseas outposts can yield unforeseen dividends. The Copenhagen legat—the FBI's liaison with Sweden, Norway, Iceland, and Finland, in addition to its host country—investigates or assists on many of the same types of crimes seen elsewhere in the world: cyber,

Left: Johannes Van Den Hoogen, FBI legal attaché in Copenhagen, at Danish National Police headquarters.

terrorism, organized crime and financial fraud. If dots from a U.S. case lead to any of the Nordic countries, the FBI can call on its partners; if the dots lead back to the U.S., agents in field offices can assist by running down leads.

In a recent child pornography case in Finland, investigators tracked obscene images to the United States. The FBI opened its own parallel case, interviewed victimized children here, and helped Finnish police lock up a criminal. That mutually beneficial cooperation is common, said Van Den Hoogen. When it comes to international fugitives, this close cooperation is paramount. In the past year, the skilled work of Swedish police officers helped to locate two fugitives sought by the FBI.

"When cooperation is built on friendships and your partners also see you care about their country, they will go to extra lengths to work with you," he said.

In Denmark, where Legat Copenhagen was established in 1999, local police know they can rely on the FBI's extensive network if a case reaches beyond its borders. "We can take advantage of your network, your relationships, your contacts," said Jens Henrik Højbjerg, commissioner of the Danish National Police, which covers the country's 12 police districts as well as its intelligence service. "And this is very, very helpful."

Denmark has a relatively low crime rate, but the region isn't immune to threats seen in lower latitudes. In 2011, a lone gunman killed 69 people at a youth camp outside Oslo, Norway. In 2008, U.S. citizen David Headley plotted a terrorist attack on a Danish newspaper on behalf of al Qaeda. Violent biker gangs are as troubling to Danish authorities as street gangs are to police in the United States. Cyber crime, meanwhile, respects no borders, a potential problem for isolated countries.

"When it comes to cyber crime, we are grateful that we have cooperation," said Commissioner Højbjerg.

Van Den Hoogen said the benefits flow both ways. "Treat your partners well and work with them and you will get stuff turned around very quickly," he said.

Scan this **QR code** with your smartphone to access related videos, or visit www.fbi.gov/legatcopenhagen.

'Serial Infector' Gets 39 Years
Linked to Hepatitis C Outbreak

The vast majority of health care professionals are dedicated individuals committed to their patients. But in a recent investigation, we came across a hospital worker who was more committed to his own selfish needs than to his patients—he knowingly put patients at risk of exposure to the hepatitis C virus so he could steal and abuse a powerful narcotic prescribed for use during medical procedures.

David Kwiatkowski—who pled guilty to a scheme to divert and obtain the controlled substance fentanyl as well as to product tampering, was sentenced earlier this month to 39 years in prison. Because of Kwiatowski's actions, at least 45 people became infected with hepatitis C, a virus that attacks the liver and may cause liver damage, liver failure, or cancer. At least one patient died as a result of the infection.

You see, Kwiatkowski himself was infected with hepatitis C. And he admitted that while employed at a New Hampshire hospital and at hospitals in several other states, he stole syringes of fentanyl prepared for patients about to undergo medical procedures, injected himself with the drug, and refilled those same syringes with saline—tainting them with his hepatitis C-positive blood—for use on unsuspecting victims. As a trained health care worker, Kwiatkowski would have known that hepatitis C, a blood-borne viral disease, is primarily transmitted by exposure to infected blood.

How the case began. In May 2012, the New Hampshire Department of Health and Human Services began a public health investigation after it was notified by an area hospital of four patients newly diagnosed with hepatitis C. Three of the individuals had been patients in the hospital's Cardiac Catheterization Laboratory (CCL), while the fourth was a CCL employee (Kwiatkowski). Although Kwiatkowski led the hospital to believe he had been previously unaware of his hepatitis C status, the investigation showed that he had known of his infection since at least 2010.

Testing confirmed that all four shared a genetically similar virus, indicating a common source of infection. Because Kwiatkowski had previously worked as a traveling technician in multiple hospitals in several states, the

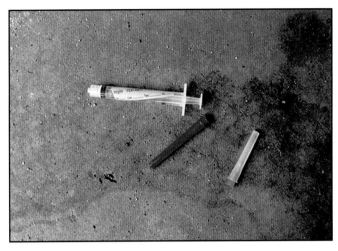

Medical syringes seized by law enforcement from inside health care worker David Kwiatkowski's car.

information about his activities was shared with those states, which began their own reviews.

The federal Centers for Disease Control and Prevention coordinated the overall public health investigation, which ruled out other possible methods of transmission and suspected that a drug diversion scheme was the source of the outbreak. During their investigation, public health authorities recommended that more than 12,000 people who may have crossed paths with Kwiatkowski in various hospitals get tested for possible hepatitis C infection.

In June 2012, the FBI's Boston Field Office opened a full criminal investigation into the outbreak...and into Kwiatkowsi. The investigation involved several search warrants and included a search of Kwiatkowski's vehicle that uncovered needles and syringes. Working with public health agencies along with other federal, state, and local law enforcement partners, we gathered evidence and interviewed dozens of people who either worked with Kwiatkowski or were patients at hospitals that employed him. By July 2012, we were able to arrest him.

According to New Hampshire U.S. Attorney John Kacavas, the 39-year sentence imposed on Kwiatkowski "ensures that this serial infector will no longer be in a position to harm innocent and vulnerable people, extinguishing once and for all the pernicious threat he posed to public health and safety."

Cyber Stalker
A Cautionary Tale About Online Romance and Revenge

A 29-year-old Michigan man was sentenced to five years in federal prison last week—the maximum allowed by law—for interstate stalking in a bizarre case of online romance gone bad.

Brian Curtis Hile traveled to San Diego from Michigan in 2011 intending to kill a woman and her boyfriend after the pair had unwittingly gotten caught up in Hile's virtual love affair.

Hile had been ensnared in a "catfish" scheme—in which a person uses social media to pretend to be someone they're not, typically to engage in misleading online romances. During the course of an Internet-only relationship that lasted two years, Hile exchanged explicit photos and romantic communications with someone he believed to be a woman. When he learned that "she" was actually a man living in South Africa, Hile became enraged and vowed to find the man who deceived him—and the woman whose images played a role in the deception.

"The woman in this case was a victim twice," said Special Agent Steve Kim in our San Diego Division. Kim, a member of the Computer and Technology Crime High-Tech Response Team—a multi-agency task force that apprehends and prosecutes criminals who use technology to prey on victims—explained that when the woman was 18 years old, she took revealing pictures of herself for personal use, never intending for them to be seen publicly. Those photos were later stolen from her online account, which she was aware of. "But she had no idea what was being done with them," Kim said.

Hile's primary target for revenge was the man who duped him, but South Africa was too far away. So using what Kim described as "circular logic," Hile went after the woman. "He knew she didn't have anything to do with the romance scam," Kim said, "but he believed she bore some responsibility. In his mind, the mere fact that those photos were used indicated that she was somehow responsible for what had happened to him."

An avid Internet user and computer gamer, Hile was determined to learn the woman's identity. He conducted an extensive online search and used hacking tools. "Eventually, he was able to hack into her e-mail account," Kim said, and compiled detailed personal information about the woman and her live-in boyfriend as well as their extended family and friends.

Armed with her address, Hile purchased a bus ticket from Michigan to San Diego to exact his revenge. Fortunately, Hile's family sensed that he was planning something and alerted authorities, which eventually led to Hile's detention in San Diego—about a mile from the woman's residence.

At the time of his arrest, he was in possession of the woman's address, telephone numbers, and information such as her favorite restaurant. He also had duct tape, zip ties, and a to-do list that included obtaining a knife and chloroform.

"Had he gotten there," Kim said, "we are convinced he would have hurt or killed the victims." Hile was found guilty by a San Diego jury in August 2013.

Kim believes this case should serve as a cautionary tale for others. When it comes to social media sites, he said, "You really have to know the people you are communicating with. If you don't absolutely know who's on the other end, you shouldn't be sending personal information or photographs. The Internet is an amazing thing," he added, "but it's also a very scary thing."

The Year in Review
A Look at FBI Cases, Part 1

The FBI worked thousands of investigations during 2013, involving everything from extremists bent on terror to cyber thieves, financial fraudsters, and murder and hostage situations. As the year comes to a close, we take our annual look back at some of the Bureau's most significant cases.

Part 1 focuses on our top investigative priority—protecting the nation from terrorist attack. We work toward that goal with our local, state, and federal law enforcement and intelligence community partners, primarily through our Joint Terrorism Task Forces around the country.

Here are some of the top terror cases of 2013, in reverse chronological order:

Airport bomb plot: A 58-year-old man was charged earlier this month with attempting to explode a car bomb at a Kansas airport as an act of jihad against the U.S. He was arrested as a result of an undercover investigation. The device provided to him by our operatives was inert and posed no danger to the public.

Attempt to join al Qaeda: A New York man was arrested in October for attempting to join al Qaeda in the Arabian Peninsula and conspiring to commit murder overseas. The 25-year-old allegedly conspired with others to travel overseas to wage violent jihad against the perceived enemies of Islam, which included the secular government in Yemen.

Material support to terrorists: Two individuals—one an American citizen—were indicted in August for conspiring to provide material support to al Qaeda groups and al Shabaab. The men were charged with attempting to provide money and recruits to three different terror organizations.

Sovereign citizen scheme: In July, the self-proclaimed president of a sovereign citizen group in Alabama was sentenced to 18 years in prison for promoting a tax fraud scheme that taught people how to defraud the IRS. He and other sovereign citizens also sent demands to all 50 U.S. governors in 2010 ordering each to resign within three days—to be replaced by a "sovereign" leader or be "removed."

Attempt to wage jihad: A Florida man was indicted in July for attempting to provide material support to

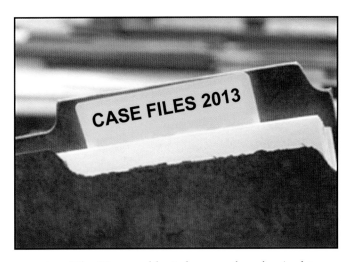

terrorists. The 19-year-old tried to travel to the Arabian Peninsula to join and fight with a violent al Qaeda group that has taken responsibility for multiple attacks on Yemeni forces, including a suicide bombing in 2012 that killed more than 100 soldiers.

Former U.S. soldier indicted: A U.S. citizen who formerly served in the Army was indicted in June for conspiring to provide material support to a foreign terrorist organization. The 30-year-old man allegedly wanted to fight alongside an al Qaeda-affiliated terrorist group in Syria.

Far-fetched terror plan: Two New York men were charged in June with conspiracy to provide material support to terrorists. Their scheme involved creating a remotely operated X-ray radiation-emitting device designed to kill people silently. Their targets were perceived enemies of Israel.

Tsarnaev charged: In April, 19-year-old Dzhokhar Tsarnaev was charged with using a weapon of mass destruction for his role in the Boston Marathon bombings. The attacks killed three people and injured more than 260 others.

Suicide bombing: An Oregon resident was charged in March for his role in a 2009 suicide bombing. The man allegedly assisted an individual who participated in the attack at the headquarters of Pakistan's intelligence service in Lahore that killed approximately 30 individuals and injured 300 others.

Bin Laden associate arrested: An associate of Osama bin Laden was arrested in March for conspiring to kill Americans. The individual held a key position in al Qaeda and appeared with bin Laden after the 9/11 attacks to threaten further attacks against the U.S.

Part 2: Cyber crime, espionage, fraud, and more (page 96)

The Year in Review
A Look at FBI Cases, Part 2

With our partners in the law enforcement and intelligence communities, the FBI worked thousands of investigations during 2013, from cyber crimes to espionage and multi-million-dollar fraud schemes. As the year draws to a close, we take a look back at some of 2013's most significant cases.

Part 1 focused on terrorism. Part 2 highlights top cases—in reverse chronological order—from the FBI's other investigative priorities:

Silk Road seizure: In October, $28 million worth of virtual money called bitcoins was seized from the owner and operator of the Silk Road website—an illegal global cyber business designed to broker criminal transactions.

Navy Yard tragedy: In September, the FBI responded to the shootings at Washington's Navy Yard and later released its findings about the shooter, Aaron Alexis, along with photos and video.

Operation Cross Country: In July, 105 juveniles were recovered—and more than 150 pimps arrested—in the seventh nationwide operation targeting underage prostitution. The three-day sweep took place in 76 cities and was carried out by the FBI in partnership with local, state, and federal law enforcement agencies and the National Center for Missing & Exploited Children as part of the Bureau's Innocence Lost National Initiative.

Health care fraud: In May, the FBI's Medicare Fraud Strike Force charged 89 individuals—including doctors, nurses, and other licensed medical professionals—for their alleged participation in Medicare fraud schemes involving approximately $223 million in false billing.

Drug trafficking, money laundering: In May, four individuals were convicted in a sophisticated conspiracy to launder millions of dollars in illicit Los Zetas drug trafficking proceeds by purchasing, training, breeding, and racing American quarter horses in the U.S.

Conspiracy to commit espionage: A former U.S. federal employee was indicted in May for conspiracy to commit espionage for Cuba. The individual allegedly helped Cuba's intelligence service recruit and insert a spy into the U.S. Defense Intelligence Agency.

Public corruption: In March, former Detroit mayor Kwame Kilpatrick, his father, and a prominent city contractor were convicted of racketeering, extortion, bribery, fraud, and tax charges related to Kilpatrick's long-running criminal enterprise while in office.

Credit card scam: In February, 18 individuals were charged for allegedly creating thousands of phony identities to steal at least $200 million in one of the largest credit card fraud schemes ever charged by the federal government.

Alabama bunker standoff: In January, a man held a 5-year-old boy captive for nearly a week in an underground bunker in Alabama. Working together with state and local law enforcement, members of the FBI's Hostage Rescue Team eventually entered the bunker and rescued the child.

Cyber crime: In January, three alleged international cyber criminals were charged in New York with creating and distributing the potent Gozi virus, which infected more than a million computers worldwide and caused tens of millions of dollars in losses.

For more information about the cases mentioned on pages 95-96, visit www.fbi.gov/yearinreview2013.

Index

Index

Index

FOREIGN COUNTERINTELLIGENCE

HISTORY

Index

Index

Index